The Art of Personal Witnessing

The Art of Personal Witnessing

by

LORNE C. SANNY

MOODY PRESS

CHICAGO

ISBN: 0-8024-0304-2

Moody Press, a ministry of the Moody Bible Institute, is
designed for education, evangelization and edification.
If we may assist you in knowing more about Christ and
the Christian life, please write us without obligation to:
Moody Press, c/o MLM, Chicago, Illinois 60610.

Printed in the United States of America

CONTENTS

FOREWORD

This book by Lorne Sanny is a significant contribution to the field of personal work.

One feature of note is the material he covers, which is the outgrowth of six years' experience on the Billy Graham team training counselors in the United States, Canada, and the British Isles.

Another is the emphasis on the spiritual life and growth of the personal worker.

A third feature is instruction in the follow-up of the new believer, which is often overlooked. The important place given to follow-up is appropriate and timely.

Mr. Sanny has the happy faculty of stating his ideas in a clear and simple manner, and he enriches his instructions with pointed illustrations.

We trust that through this book many of God's people will become more effective witnesses for Christ.

JOHN I. PATON

1

YOU CAN WITNESS EFFECTIVELY TO INDIVIDUALS

HAVE YOU EVER KNOWN THE JOY of witnessing to a friend about Christ and seeing that person's life transformed by the power of God? If so, you know that that is one of the greatest thrills that can come to a Christian. A man who all his adult lifetime gave himself to witnessing to individuals said, "Even if I were utterly selfish and had no care for anything but my own happiness, I would choose, if I might, under God, to be a soul winner." Real happiness comes to the person who witnesses to another about the Lord Jesus and sees that one pass from death to life.

What a privilege it is to see light come into a life to replace darkness, to see a soul freed from the bondage of Satan and come into the liberty that is in the Lord Jesus Christ! Did you ever have this privilege of pointing someone to the Saviour and seeing that one respond to the work of the Spirit of God? Have you also had the added pleasure of watching that person grow in the Lord and begin to witness to other individuals?

CHRIST'S PROMISE TO MAKE YOU A FISHER OF MEN

We can all know that joy and have that privilege. God intended that we should. We can witness effectively to individuals, for the Lord Jesus promised that He would make us fishers of men. One day when the Lord was walking by the Sea of Galilee He saw two brothers, Simon called Peter, and Andrew his brother, casting a net into the sea, for they were fishermen. He said to them, "Follow me, and I will make you fishers of men" (Mt 4:19). The Lord Jesus commands us to follow Him and promises that when we do, He will make us fishers of men. What He has promised, that He will perform.

We may not be like Peter, who preached one day and three thousand were added to the Church. We can be like Andrew, however, who after he had been brought to the Saviour, found his brother, Peter, and brought him to the Lord Jesus. Peter fished with a net, so to speak, and caught large numbers. Andrew fished with a pole and a line, catching one fish at a time. We may not be called upon to preach to great multitudes or even to groups, yet we can witness effectively to individuals one by one—the pole and line method. What a privilege that can be! We, like Andrew, might lead someone to the Lord, and that one, in turn, might lead thousands.

Sunday school teacher Edward Kimball led a young man to Christ years ago. Kimball is practically unknown today, but most of us know about that salesman he led to the Lord in a shoe store— D. L. Moody, who later became the great evangelist. It is well to remember that seven of the twelve apostles were won through personal work.

The Lord Jesus did not command us to be fishers of men, however. He commanded us to follow Him; and then He promised, as the result of our response, to make us fishers of men. As someone once said, "Responsibility—the response is to come from us, and the ability will come from Him."

We can witness effectively for Christ to other individuals, our friends, neighbors, and acquaintances, because He has promised to make each of us a fisher of men.

THE LORD OUR EXAMPLE IN PERSONAL WITNESSING

The Lord Jesus, though He taught large groups, is also our Example in personal witnessing. As we read the account of His life in the gospels, we find that nineteen different times He taught just one person. Take, for example, the woman at the well. The incident is recorded in John, chapter four. At noon He sat on the edge of the well, and a woman who had had five husbands came to draw water. The narrative tells how He led her step by step to faith in Himself, and then how she in turn brought the villagers to hear Him so that they, too, might believe in Him.

Another day He came into a town, looked up into a tree, saw Zacchaeus, a tax gatherer, and said, "Come down, Zacchaeus, for to day I must abide at thy house. . . . This day is salvation come to this house" (Lk 19:5, 9).

At another time a religious leader, Nicodemus by name, came to the Lord Jesus by night, and the Lord dealt with him personally. So we have both the promise of the Lord Jesus that He will make us effective witnesses to individuals, and the example of how to do it.

THE GREATEST WORK GOD PERMITS MEN TO DO

To witness to the saving grace of Christ is the greatest work that God permits men to do. The Lord Jesus said of Himself, "The Son of man is come to seek and to save that which was lost" (Lk 19:10). He does all the saving and most of the seeking; but the latter He wants to do through us. Being a fisher of men, therefore, is one of the greatest privileges that we can have. It not only is the greatest work that God permits us to do—to colabor with Him in seeking the souls of men—it is also the hardest. Satan will bitterly oppose something so effective as personal witnessing.

Do not we, who call ourselves ordinary lay Christians, make a mistake when we feel that this work of evangelism is to be done by a select few, such as Bible school or seminary students or missionaries or pastors? Such a view is wrong because the Bible indicates that every saved person is to be a soldier; every child of God is to be a witness for the Lord Jesus. That includes you and me.

WITNESSING, AN ART TO BE LEARNED

We may not be talented. We may lack experience. Perhaps we are afraid; but remember that witnessing for Christ either to groups or individuals is like anything else—it is an art to be learned, and it requires certain things.

First, it takes personal preparation. We need to be prepared to have something to say, to know what to say, and to have boldness with which to say it. A heart of love and a Christlike life to back it up are essentials. Furthermore, we need a knowledge of how to approach a person who is seemingly uninterested or even hostile to the things of God.

In addition to all of that, we need to know how to tell the Gospel story simply and forcefully, and how to care for the one whom we have led to the Lord.

The purpose of these messages is to help Christians to prepare for, and actually do, personal witnessing. The subject matter given and the suggestions made are the outgrowth of six years of experience in helping believers all over the country. For six years it was my privilege, as a member of the Billy Graham team, to train counselors and personal work counselors in various parts of this country, in Canada, and in the British Isles.

During those years I gave considerable thought to this question: If I were to take an average group of Christians and had only two things to teach them in order to make them the most effective personal workers for Christ in the least amount of time, what would those two things be? I believe that I know what they are, and among other things, they constitute a large part of the information contained in this series of messages on personal witnessing.

Even though you are totally inexperienced, if you will follow these lessons and do the homework assigned for each, you will find yourself better equipped and more encouraged and confident to engage in witnessing for Christ to individuals with whom God brings you in contact.

THE FIRST QUESTION

The first question I would like to ask you is, Are you following the Lord Jesus in the sense of Matthew 4:19, "Follow me, and I will make you fishers of men"? It is obvious that we cannot follow Him if we have not first met Him as our Saviour. Do you know Him in this way? Can you join the apostle Paul in saying, "I know whom I have believed, and am persuaded that he is able to keep that which I have committed unto him against that day" (2 Ti 1:12)? Do we have a rock-ribbed assurance and certainty of our life in Jesus Christ?

I grew up in Sunday school and church, but somehow or other the Gospel did not mean much to me. I did not actually question the Bible, nor did I disbelieve in the Lord Jesus Christ; but at that time I did not receive Him as my Saviour.

Later, when I was a freshman in college, I walked into the back of a little church one Sunday night. The message I heard left an indelible impression upon my mind. I saw that I not only needed to know the facts about the Lord Jesus—how He died on the cross to take my sins away—but that I must receive Him as my own personal Saviour.

At first I thought, *Well, I'm a Christian. I was born in America. I've tried to live a good life.* As the weeks and the months went by I became less sure of my position. One night I lay awake in my bed thinking seriously about the matter. I said to myself: *I'm not certain I'm a Christian. If I died I don't know where I would go.* After a while I decided to make certain, and slipped out of bed, got on my knees, and asked Jesus Christ to come into my heart. It was a definite act of faith on my part. There was no emotional upheaval. That night I became a new creature in Christ. Life has been a day by day joyous experience ever since.

Do you know Him as your Saviour? If not, ask Him to come in and take over your heart and life, and He will, because He has promised.

The next thing is, if we are going to be effective in personal witnessing, we must have a working knowledge of the Scriptures. Personal witnessing is a hand-to-hand spiritual conflict; therefore, we must use spiritual weapons.

Assignments

(Note: These assignments and questions are added as guides to your private study and review.)

1. Study carefully chapter 14, "Beginning With Christ" (p. 110).

2. List as many reasons as you can why you should do personal witnessing.
3. Why is personal witnessing likely to be difficult?
4. What assurances do you have that God will help you in individual witnessing?

2

THE PLACE OF THE BIBLE IN PERSONAL WITNESSING

THE PARABLE OF THE SOWER is found in the eighth chapter of Luke. There we learn that when the sower sowed seed, some fell by the wayside, some on stony ground, some on thorny ground, and some on good ground. In the interpretation of the story, the Lord Jesus said that the seed is the Word of God.

IMPORTANCE OF THE BIBLE IN PERSONAL WORK

In witnessing to others about Christ, God's Word is the seed we are to sow. This is confirmed by 1 Peter 1:23: "Being born again, not of corruptible seed, but of incorruptible, by the word of God, which liveth and abideth forever." It is clearly evident, then, that since the Spirit of God uses the incorruptible seed of the Word of God in the fertile soil of the heart in order to produce the new birth, no one can be saved without that Word. This also follows: any person who wants to be a successful witness for Christ, must learn to be skillful in the use of the Bible, for in personal witnessing, it is the sower's seed.

SEED AND BREAD

According to Isaiah 55:10-11, this same Word which is seed to the sower becomes bread to the eater. Such is the function of the Word after a person comes to know Christ as Saviour. It becomes food for his soul. The Scripture says, "As newborn babes, desire the sincere milk of the word, that ye may grow thereby" (1 Pe 2:2). To become equipped for effective personal witnessing, therefore, we must come to know the Scriptures.

THE BIBLE AND THE WAY OF SALVATION

The Bible, and the Bible only, shows the way of salvation. Note these significant words in 2 Timothy 3:15: "And that from a child thou hast known the holy scriptures, which are able to make thee wise unto salvation through faith which is in Christ Jesus." This needs no further explanation. The Holy Scriptures are able to make us wise unto salvation through faith which is in Christ Jesus. They point us to Him.

THE ONLY EFFECTIVE WEAPON

We have indicated that the Bible is the only effective weapon for this spiritual conflict. That this is so, is clear as we reflect for a moment on the condition of a person outside of Christ. Consider the words of Acts 26:18. Paul was sent to the Gentiles with the Gospel in order to "open their eyes, and to turn them from darkness to light, and from the power of Satan unto God." A person outside of Christ is blind, in darkness, and under the power of Satan.

These same facts are presented in 2 Corinthians 4:3-4, where we read, "If our gospel be hid, it is hid to them that are lost; in whom the god of this world hath blinded the minds of them which believe not, lest the light of the glorious gospel of Christ, who is the image of God, should shine unto them." Here we see that the enemy, Satan, has blinded the minds of them which believe not. He has blinded them concerning a particular message— the Gospel. How are we to give sight to the blind? How can we bring a person from darkness to light, from the power of Satan unto God? Will any argument suffice that you or I have? Definitely not! In order to wage a spiritual battle, to engage in spiritual warfare, we must use spiritual weapons. But what are they? The answer is found in Ephesians

6:17: "Take the helmet of salvation, and the sword of the Spirit, which is the word of God."

A good illustration of how this weapon should be used in spiritual warfare is found in the fourth chapter of Matthew. There the account of the temptation of the Lord Jesus in the wilderness is given. The record is, "And when the tempter came to him, he said, If thou be the Son of God, command that these stones be made bread. But he answered and said, It is written, Man shall not live by bread alone, but by every word that proceedeth out of the mouth of God" (Mt 4:3-4). In meeting this attack, the Lord Jesus quoted from Deuteronomy, the eighth chapter. Someone has said, "When dealing with the devil, don't argue, quote."

This is also true in effective personal witnessing. We must use the Word of God, the spiritual weapon that has been placed at our disposal, and we do that by showing what it says. Suppose someone were to say, "I don't believe the Bible, so don't quote the Bible to me." Would that person's lack of faith make the Bible any less the sword of the Spirit? Do you think for one moment that God who created heaven and earth and spoke this Word cannot use it to penetrate that unbelieving heart?

Read what God declared through Jeremiah: "Is not my word like as a fire? saith the LORD; and like a hammer that breaketh the rock in pieces?" (Jer 23:29). The Spirit of God will use the Word to penetrate a heart in a miraculous way. It is through the Scriptures that He first brings conviction of sin and shows the need of the Saviour. The same Book shows convicted sinners that Christ is the Saviour they need. It shows them how to receive Him as Saviour, and answers the difficulties that hinder them from receiving Him. Assurance of salvation also comes by means of it. The Bible, then, is an indispensable weapon in personal witnessing.

MEMORIZING SCRIPTURE FOR EFFECTIVE WITNESSING

How are we to come to know the Bible? Is there one means that is more effective than another to equip us quickly for effective witnessing? There is —memorizing Scripture, hiding portions of Bible in our hearts. This will fill our hearts with something to say, and we will experience what is said in Jeremiah 20:9: "Then I said, I will not make mention of him, nor speak any more in his name. But his word was in mine heart as a burning fire shut up in my bones, and I was weary with forbearing, and I could not stay." He will not only fill our hearts with something to say, but He will permit us to speak with confidence.

Another benefit is that through the Word hidden in the heart we can have victory over sin in our own lives. It pays to memorize Scripture.

ASSIGNMENTS

1. Reread chapter 14, "Beginning with Christ."
2. Memorize 1 John 5:11-12. Review this verse every day until it becomes a part of you.
3. What do you feel are the most important things necessary by way of preparation for effective personal witnessing?
4. List some reasons why the Bible is indispensable not only to effective witnessing but to living a victorious Christian life.

3

WHY MEMORIZE SCRIPTURE?

FOR USE IN PERSONAL WITNESSING, one of the quickest and most effective ways to gain a working knowledge of the Bible is to commit Scripture verses to memory. Remember also that when we are witnessing for Christ, it is not our arguments which God has promised to bless but His Word. Proof of this is found in John 3:34. It says, "For he whom God hath sent speaketh the words of God." This was spoken of Christ, but it applies to us when witnessing. If God sends us to a neighbor or to a friend to speak to that person about His Son, we should speak the words of God. How can we speak them, however, if we do not know them? By memorizing Scripture portions we will have something on our heart which we will want to share with someone else.

A friend of mine who went to India a few years ago tells of a conversation he had with some missionaries there. They told him in the course of their talk that they were unable to get the Christians of India, at least in their locality, to witness. This friend of mine said to them: "Have you ever tried getting them to memorize Scripture?"

"No," they answered, "we have not."

My friend then asked: "Would you try?"

This they agreed to do, and happy results followed. After a few weeks, when time was given in a meeting for testimonies, the young national believers got up and quoted one of the verses of Scripture which they had recently committed to memory. As the weeks went by, they not only stood up and repeated verses, but they also shared with those in the service the message God had given from those particular portions of Scripture. It was not long after that until these same Christians were witnessing to their friends and neighbors. Having the Scriptures on the tables of their hearts, they had something to say.

One reason so many Christians do not witness is that they are frustrated. They do not know what to say. But when we memorize Scripture we are able to say, "Thus saith the Lord," and say it with confidence. David said in Psalm 119:42, "So shall I have wherewith to answer him that reproacheth me: for I trust in thy word." The Word of God through our lips will be like an arrow which will pierce the heart of a person for Christ.

Let me give a personal word at this point. For me, the memorizing of Scripture has paid greater dividends for the time spent than any other form of Scripture instruction. It may be difficult at first for some to memorize, but it can be done.

FOR VICTORY OVER SATAN

We must memorize Scripture so that we can have victory over Satan. This was clearly demonstrated by the Lord Jesus in the way He used Bible passages to meet the attacks of the enemy. We saw this in the preceding lesson. The record as found in Matthew is, "And when the tempter came to him, he said, If thou be the Son of God, command that these stones be made bread. But he answered and said, It is written, Man shall not live by bread alone, but by every word that proceedeth out of the mouth of God" (Mt 4:3-4). The Lord Jesus quoted from Deuteronomy 8:3.

Defeated at one point, Satan attacked at another. "Then the devil taketh him up into the holy city, and setteth him on a pinnacle of the temple" (Mt 4:5). And in this case, the enemy himself quoted Scripture, but there are at least two things wrong with what he did. In the first place, he misquoted. He left out a phrase from Psalm 91:11-12 (the part from which he quoted), and in so doing changed the meaning of the passage. In the second place, remember that the Word of God is the sword of the Spirit, and Satan has no part in the work of the Holy Spirit. It makes a difference who uses the Scriptures. The Lord Jesus in reply to the devil quoted Deuteronomy 6:16: "Thou shalt not tempt the Lord thy God."

By His example, our Saviour taught us that in order to meet the attacks of Satan, we must use Scripture.

In the little book called, "Beginning with Christ" there is a part to be read and studied, and in the back four verses of Scripture to be memorized. The first three of those verses are calculated to help you meet the three most common attacks of the evil one on a young Christian.

The first attack is an attempt to get the believer to doubt his salvation. Victory comes in committing 1 John 5:11-12 to memory. The Spirit of God will recall this to your mind to give you confidence and assurance. The second attack of Satan is to bring temptation. If you have already memorized 1 Corinthians 10:13, that verse will be like a sword which the Holy Spirit can use in your heart to give you victory over sin. In the third place, in the event that Satan should trip us up, there is 1 John 1:9, which says: "If we confess our sins, he is faithful and just to forgive us our sins, and to cleanse us from all unrighteousness."

FOR VICTORY OVER SIN

By carefully fulfilling the assignments which conclude each lesson you will soon have a number of such verses committed to memory. Furthermore, you will soon see demonstrated in your own life how these verses will be brought to your mind by the Holy Spirit to meet the attacks of Satan. The psalmist said, "Thy Word have I hid in mine heart that I might not sin against thee" (Ps 119:11).

When I was a young Christian, I desired to have victory in my own life and prayed for victory, but somehow or other it did not come. Then a man by the name of Dawson Trotman, who founded the Navigators' work, got me started hiding the Word of God in the tables of my heart. As the months and the years passed, I saw that the Spirit of God used the Word to give me victory. Since that time, it has been my privilege to teach a large number of people in personal work and personal counseling, and in all that time I have yet to meet a Christian who is living a consistent, victorious life who is not getting into the Word of God. Victory cannot be had without the Word.

The Word hidden in our hearts will not in itself give us victory, but we will make that Word available to the Holy Spirit. Then when our lives and the hidden Word are energized by prayer, we will find that we have increasing victory.

FOR EFFECTIVE WITNESSING

I know of nothing that will enable us to be always ready to give an answer to every man, more than committing Scripture verses to memory.

Read what Proverbs 22:20-21 says. "Have not I written to thee excellent things in counsels and knowledge, that I might make thee know the certainty of the words of truth; that thou mightest answer the words of truth to them that send unto thee?" Persons who will want spiritual help or advice from us will want to be answered by the words of truth—the Bible. We will find that as we commit Scripture passages to memory, the Holy Spirit will call to our remembrance just the verse or verses needed.

A few years ago a businessman came to see me. In telling me about himself, he said, "I tried this, and it failed. I tried that, and it did not succeed; then I tried something else, and that didn't prosper."

After he had talked for a little while, the Spirit of God brought a verse of Scripture to my mind which I read to him.

He then asked me, "Where did you find that verse? I've been looking for twenty years for a verse like that."

Here is what I read to him. "This book of the law shall not depart out of thy mouth; but thou shalt meditate therein day and night, that thou mayest observe to do according to all that is written therein: for then thou shalt make thy way prosperous, and then thou shalt have good success" (Jos 1:8). The Spirit of God will call such verses to our minds; we will not quote them indiscriminately but selectively.

ASSIGNMENTS

1. Reread chapter 14, "Beginning With Christ."
2. Memorize 1 Corinthians 10:13. Review it until it becomes a part of you.
3. According to the chapter "Beginning With Christ," what are the three main attacks of Satan on a young Christian?
4. According to 1 Corinthians 10:13, of what four things may we always be sure when we are tempted?

4

YOU CAN MEMORIZE IF YOU KNOW HOW!

WITNESSING IS THE RESPONSIBILITY of every Christian. It is not restricted to certain select people such as full-time Christian workers or missionaries, but every child of God is called to be a "fisher of men." We do not witness more often, chiefly because we are not prepared. Moreover, we must pay a price for this.

Some years ago, there was a sailor on the U.S.S. *West Virginia* who had joined the navy with the idea of saving up enough money in order to enter seminary after his period of service was finished. In the navy he lost track of his objective and drifted away from the Lord. A Christian woman who knew him prayed for him daily. She knew another young man, Dawson Trotman by name, whom God was using in a great way. She asked Mr. Trotman if he would speak with this young sailor about spiritual matters.

Mr. Trotman agreed to meet Les Spencer at the navy landing. From there they drove in Mr. Trotman's car to the top of one of the hills near Long Beach, California, to talk. No sooner had they begun their discussion than a policeman walked up to the window of the car and wanted to know what they were doing. Mr. Trotman held up a Bible. The policeman first looked at the Bible and then at the sailor and began to ask questions.

For an hour, Mr. Trotman answered the policeman's questions by turning first to one Scripture portion and then to another. At the end of that time, the policeman knelt down and received Jesus Christ as his personal Saviour.

As the young sailor and Mr. Trotman drove down the hill, the sailor said to Mr. Trotman, "I would give my right arm to be able to do what you did tonight—just to lead a person to Christ."

Mr. Trotman told him, "You can do what I did tonight, Les. It won't cost you your right arm, but it will cost you something by way of preparation, study, the memorizing of Scripture, and a strong prayer-life."

Mr. Trotman invited Les Spencer over to his home a couple of nights a week, and it was not long before Les, in turn, was used in another life.

That was the beginning of the Navigators work. It cost something, and it will cost us something, too. But if we have a genuine desire to be used as fishers of men, and are willing to pay the price, God will use us. We will need a working knowledge of the Bible, and one of the best ways to acquire that for effective personal witnessing is through memorizing Scripture verses.

As we pointed out in Chapter 3, this will give you something to say, and you will have the confidence that you are speaking not your own words but the words of God. Furthermore, it is through this means that the Spirit of God will enable you to have victory over sin and Satan. At the same time you will be ready always to give an answer to every man who asks you a reason for the hope that is in you.

Too often we think of a verse of Scripture that we should have used the day before. Scripture memorizing will take the Word of God and put it right on our lips, like an arrow ready to fly into the heart of the individual with whom we are dealing.

DIRECTION FINDER

There are several other reasons why it would be very valuable for us, regardless of the effort it costs, to commit Bible passages to memory. One of them is this: It is a fast way to come to know our way about the Bible. Well-chosen Scripture verses committed to memory become like signposts that will direct our way in the Word.

For instance, we know that the story of Nicodemus is in John 3, because we have memorized John 3:16. Or we know that the story of the good Samaritan is in Luke 10, because we have committed to memory Luke 10:33-34.

MEDITATION ON THE WORD

What a rich source of blessing there is in meditating on the Scriptures! A great aid to this is the memorizing of verses. We read in the Psalms: "But his delight is in the law of the LORD; and in his law doth he meditate day and night. And he shall be like a tree planted by the rivers of water, that bringeth forth his fruit in his season; his leaf also shall not wither; and whatsoever he doeth shall prosper" (Ps 1:2-3). This is the way to prosper, and the goal is made easier for us when we have the Word where we can recall it to mind at any time—walking down the street, before going to sleep at night, and when we wake up in the morning.

COMMAND TO MEMORIZE SCRIPTURE

There is still another passage which lends strong

encouragement to our memorizing of Scripture. What is the greatest commandment in the Bible? That question was asked of the Lord Jesus, and His answer was, "Thou shalt love the Lord thy God with all thy heart, and with all thy soul, and with all thy strength, and with all thy mind" (Lk 10:27). He quoted directly from Deuteronomy 6:5; and Deuteronomy 6:6 says, "And these words, which I command thee this day, shall be in thine heart." What better way to get them into our hearts than to commit them to memory?

This same idea is suggested in verse seven. "And thou shalt teach them diligently unto thy children, and thou shalt talk of them when thou sittest in thine house, and when thou walkest by the way, and when thou liest down, and when thou risest up." In other words, our lives should be saturated with the Word of God.

ABILITY TO MEMORIZE

Many persons, when encouraged to memorize Scripture, say, "I have a poor memory." The fact is that most of us have poor memories. Yet I have seen thousands of people successfully memorize Scripture, though most of them had poor memories. On the other hand, our memories may be better than we think. For instance, I have heard it said that two women who have not seen each other for some time can meet on a street corner, talk for fifteen or twenty minutes, and then go home and recount the entire conversation to their respective husbands, almost verbatim. That takes a good memory.

Psychologically, we can memorize. All things being equal, the older we become, the better our memory, and not the worse. Our minds are essentially associating machines, and memory is quickened by tying a new thought to an old. For that reason, the more knowledge and background and experience we have, the more we have with which to tie in a new verse of Scripture. The problem is not so much our memories as it is our poor concentration while working on the verses. Many old people have committed the verses to memory that are in the memory packets. Among them is a lady of seventy-two, another aged seventy-eight, a man eighty-four, and a man ninety.

We must apply the rules of memory, and one of these is review. Some of you say, "I can get a verse memorized today, but tomorrow I will forget it."

In that case, you did not really memorize it; you only repeated it. A verse is not really memorized until it sticks in one's mind, and that takes time and review—daily review. We should review a verse once today, once tomorrow, once the next

day, and so on for a number of weeks until it becomes a part and parcel of our being.

Some may object by saying, "I don't have time
to memorize."

The memorizing of Scripture does not take time,
it saves time. We can do it while washing dishes.
Why not place a verse of Scripture on the window
sill in back of the sink? Or the men can place it on
the mirror, while they shave. If the Lord wants us
to commit Scripture to memory, is it not reasonable
to think that He will also give us the needed ability
to do it? Of course He will!

How to Memorize

Here are two factors to remember in memorizing
Scripture. First, have a definite plan. Learn so
many verses per week. We have started with one
each lesson as part of the homework. Now we
should be able to memorize two verses—the next
two in "Beginning with Christ": 1 John 1:9, and
John 16:24. These verses are shorter than some of
the others. Second, be consistent. Work on your
verses every day, and if possible, early in the day.

Tools are an aid in the memorizing of Scripture.
That is why the chapters "Beginning With Christ"
and "Going On With Christ" have been added.
These are reprinted from two booklets, bearing the
same titles, which are published by the Navigators,

Colorado Springs, Colorado. "Beginning With Christ" contains four and "Going On With Christ" contains eight Scriptures to be memorized. Both booklets also include information on "The Topical Memory System Correspondence Course," with instructions on how to enroll. Should you do so, you will find this to be one of the best investments you have ever made.

Assignments

1. Memorize 1 John 1:9 and John 16:24.
2. What to you are the three most important reasons for committing Scripture passages to memory?
3. Write out briefly your plan for systematically committing Scripture verses to memory.
4. List three of your greatest problems with memorizing Scripture, and indicate how you feel that you can overcome them.

5

THE REAL BASIS FOR
WITNESSING

WE HAVE SEEN that memorizing certain key passages of Scripture is one of two things needed to make Christians the most effective witnesses for Christ in the least amount of time. In the account of Paul's conversion in Acts 22, we find the second thing needed.

PERSONAL RELATIONSHIP WITH CHRIST

The Scripture states that following his meeting with the Lord on the road to Damascus, Paul, then Saul, went into that city and stayed in a house in the street called Straight.

God sent Ananias to heal Saul of his blindness and to tell him what his lifework would be. After saying, "Brother Saul, receive thy sight" (Ac 22:13), Ananias declared, "The God of our fathers hath chosen thee, that thou shouldest know his will, and see that Just One, and shouldest hear the voice of his mouth. For thou shalt be his witness unto all men of what thou hast seen and heard" (Ac 22: 14-15).

Why did God choose Paul? Some no doubt will say, "To witness concerning Christ." But these verses show that witnessing was not primary but secondary.

Read them again. Ananias said to Paul, "The God of our fathers hath chosen thee." For what? First, "That thou shouldest know his will"; second, "and see that Just One"—the Lord Jesus Christ; third, "And shouldest hear the voice of his mouth." Then following these three is this fourth and last thing: "Thou shalt be his witness unto all men of what thou hast seen and heard." From this we see that witnessing has to do with the person of the Lord Jesus Christ. We must first of all know Christ as Saviour, else how can we make Him real to another person? As the Lord Jesus said in John 3:11, "We speak that we do know, and testify that we have seen." The apostle John wrote: "These things have I written unto you that believe on the name of the Son of God; that ye may know that ye have eternal life" (1 John 5:13). We must first have a personal relationship with Jesus Christ through faith; then we live out the Christian life in fellowship with Christ.

Consider once more that passage in Acts 22. Where do we find God's will? In and through the Bible. How is it possible for us to see the Just One, the Lord Jesus Christ? Again it is in and through His Word, as the Holy Spirit reveals Him to us. Where do we hear His voice? He speaks through the Scriptures. Only after we have taken time to see Him and to hear what He has to say, can we witness to others of what we have seen and heard.

Someone has said that witnessing for Christ is simply taking a good look at the Lord, and then going out and telling people of what we have seen.

PERSONAL FELLOWSHIP WITH CHRIST

John wrote in his first epistle: "That which we have seen and heard declare we unto you, that ye also may have fellowship with us: and truly our fellowship is with the Father, and with his Son Jesus Christ" (1 John 1:3). Thus we are to share with others what we have seen and heard. A personal witness always points to Christ. He tells others and shares with them what he has seen of Christ and has heard from Christ.

Such a witness has something to say that is real and alive and penetrates the heart. Witnessing is more than sharing theological or doctrinal views with someone else. It is witnessing concerning a Person. Our Lord said in Acts 1:8, "But ye shall receive power, after that the Holy Ghost is come upon you: and ye shall be witnesses unto me." We are to be witnesses unto the person of the Lord Jesus Christ. That is true witnessing, but none of us can witness in that way unless we take time daily to gaze on the Lord Jesus and to hear the voice of His mouth. We cannot get a clear picture of Him by taking fleeting glimpses. We must take time to look steadfastly at Him and to listen to His voice.

The psalmist said, "One thing have I desired of the LORD, that will I seek after; that I may dwell in the house of the LORD all the days of my life, to behold the beauty of the LORD, and to enquire in his temple" (Ps 27:4). To behold the beauty of the Lord is to see how wonderful He is. To inquire in His temple is to listen to what He has to say. Do we take time each day to look and to listen?

Again the psalmist said, "When thou saidst, Seek ye my face; my heart said unto thee, Thy face, LORD, will I seek" (Ps 27:8). Is that our response? If it is, then we will find that we have a true basis for witnessing concerning the person of the Lord Jesus Christ. But not only that, we will find that the time set aside for listening and looking—often called the quiet time—will not only give us something to share about what we have seen and heard but will also give us the boldness to say it.

A good example of such boldness is described in

Acts 4:13: "Now when they saw the boldness of Peter and John, and perceived that they were unlearned and ignorant men, they marvelled; and they took knowledge of them, that they had been with Jesus." The members of the Sanhedrin were amazed when they saw Peter and John. The Jewish leaders were astonished, and several things amazed them; one was the boldness of the apostles. Boldness is not rudeness. Boldness in this connection simply means unembarrassed freedom of speech. Why does it seem so difficult to talk about Jesus Christ? We can talk about world conditions, sports, and other affairs of life without difficulty. Yet, when the name of Jesus Christ is mentioned at work or by the neighbors, a flush of embarrassment comes over our face, and our tongue seems to get thick. The reason lies in our not knowing the Lord very well. We have not taken time to be with Him. According to this passage in Acts 4, Peter and John had been with Jesus. That is what gave them that unembarrassed freedom of speech. Is it not true that we like to talk about someone whom we really know and love?

If we are going to have boldness to talk about Christ, we need to get to know Him better. That means we must spend time with Him, to gaze upon Him, and to hear the voice of His mouth. Not only will we have something to share, but it

will be real and alive. Moreover, when we take
time to meet with the Lord, there will be a Christ-
likeness about us as we do personal work. There
was something about Peter and John which indicated that they had been with Jesus. Is that true
of us? It will be, if we take time every day to
be with the Lord Jesus—a quiet time set aside to
meditate on His Word and to talk to Him through
prayer. This will bring a change in us. We will
become more like the Lord Jesus. "But we all, with
open face beholding as in a glass the glory of the
Lord, are changed into the same image from glory
to glory, even as by the Spirit of the Lord" (2 Co
3:18).

How do we get to know a friend better? By
spending time with him. We get acquainted with
another person by exchanging ideas and sharing
experiences. In other words, we fellowship together.

So it is with Christ. He talks to us through His
Word. In it He tells us who He is and what He
does. That is why you should spend a little time
every day, reading, studying, and memorizing
Scripture. You enter into fellowship with Him
through obeying Him and spending time with Him
in prayer.

Set aside ten, fifteen, twenty minutes, or perhaps
a longer time to fellowship with Him every day.

That is absolutely imperative and basic if you are to be an effective personal witness for Christ.

ASSIGNMENTS

1. Read "Going On With Christ."
2. Memorize Psalm 119:9, 11.
3. Write a brief paragraph on how you know that you have eternal life.
4. What are some of the main reasons why you should have a daily time set aside for personal fellowship with Christ?

6

HOW TO HAVE A QUIET TIME

THE CHRISTIAN LIFE centers in the person of the Lord Jesus Christ. We come to know Him as Saviour by a personal act of faith whereby we receive Him into our hearts and lives. Then the Christian life is lived by faith, in fellowship with Him. Through this He is made real to us personally, and because of this personal knowledge we want to tell others about Him. Unembarrassed freedom of speech will be ours, that boldness to talk to others courteously and kindly about Christ. Furthermore, our fellowship with Christ will enable us to have the Christlike life to support our spoken witness.

A DEFINITE TIME

How do we go about having a time of fellowship each day with the Lord? For help on this, look at Daniel 6:10-11, which we will use as a key passage on the subject of the quiet time. The background to this story is that certain government rulers, who

46

were envious of Daniel, persuaded King Darius to sign a decree to the effect that if anyone prayed to anyone other than the king during the next thirty days, that person would be thrown into the den of lions.

> Now when Daniel knew that the writing was signed, he went into his house; and his windows being open in his chamber toward Jerusalem, he kneeled upon his knees three times a day, and prayed, and gave thanks before his God, as he did aforetime. Then these men assembled, and found Daniel praying and making supplication before his God.

There are several things that we can learn from this incident in Daniel's life. One is that he had a definite time set aside for prayer. In his case, it was three times a day. That may not be possible for us, but one thing is certain, we ought to have a definite time set aside each day in which we meet with the Lord Jesus Christ.

The best time of day for any one of us depends upon our own program and schedule. But for most of us, early in the day before breakfast is to be preferred. Then we can quiet our own hearts before the Lord and get direction from His Word for that day. He is able to nourish us and to strengthen us and to direct us so that we will honor and glorify Him in every activity throughout the day.

In order to get that time we, no doubt, will need to get up a little earlier. This is not hard to figure. What is needed is to decide how long we want to spend in the quiet time and get up just that much earlier each morning. If you are not in the habit of having a devotional period, I suggest fifteen minutes a day, each morning before breakfast. Some who have been doing this for years, spend perhaps a half hour or an hour; but for one just beginning, the shorter time is better. When that is packed full and is rich with blessing, then you should increase the time to twenty minutes. Use the shorter period at first, and let the time increase as the Lord directs.

What is the secret for getting up in the morning? There is no mystery here. It is simply getting to bed at night. Most of us will agree that at night we putter around the house, doing this little thing and that, but not accomplishing much. The subtle battle is in getting to bed at a reasonable hour. Here we must win if we are to get adequate rest and get up in the morning and meet the Lord and be strong for the day.

One thing is very important—whatever we do, we must be consistent in our quiet time. It is a great deal better to get fifteen minutes every day than an hour on an occasional day. The Lord is not going to be angry with us, so to speak, if we miss that time in the morning; nor does it necessarily mean that the day will go bad. To me it is something like the climate and the weather. The weather will vary from day to day, but the climate is the overall average. Our devotional life or our quiet time may vary a bit from day to day with the circumstances of our life, but the overall average should be a consistent time set aside daily for fellowship with the Lord Jesus.

A Definite Place

The second thing we notice about Daniel is that he had a definite place for prayer. The place chosen should be one where we can be alone, if possible. The Lord Jesus, in order to be alone, went to great lengths at times. For example, in Matthew 14:23 we read, "And when he had sent the multitudes away, he went up into a mountain apart to pray: and when the evening was come, he was there alone."

We need to get alone and away from distractions. I do not know where that would be for each of you. It may be that there is some place around your home, in the living room, or even in the basement, which you can use.

In our home, I cleared a corner in the storage section of our garage, put a piece of rug on the cement floor, added a chair, and thus made a place to which I could go in the morning for prayer. If

the weather is pleasant, perhaps a nearby park or
a field, or even the family car would answer the
purpose. The essential thing is to find a place
where we can be alone for this quiet time.

A Simple Method

After we have a definite time and a definite
place, we ought to have a simple method. First of
all, begin with the Word of God. It is His Word
which nourishes the soul as the Lord Jesus declared
when He quoted from Deuteronomy: "Man shall
not live by bread alone, but by every word that
proceedeth out of the mouth of God." So we need
to use our Bibles.

Perhaps it would be well to read through the
gospel of John, a chapter each morning. As we
read, we should ask God to speak to our hearts so
that we will see the person of Christ. We should
also pray for truth that we can apply to our own
lives. It is far better to follow a definite plan of
this kind than to use the hunt and peck system
with a portion from one part of the Bible one day
and another part the next day. Whatever study
plan we follow, it should be something which is
consistent and systematic.

It would be well, too, for us to have a notebook
with us, so that we might jot down some of the
things which God brings to our hearts from the

Word each day. He will always apply some truth to our lives and give help in the light of the needs we face. For myself, if I were spending fifteen minutes in a quiet time, I believe that I would take seven or eight minutes for meditation in the Bible. For a thirty-minute quiet time, possibly fifteen or eighteen minutes should be spent in meditation on some portion of Scripture. Following this, we should go to prayer.

What should we do when we pray? Here are five things which will help us. First of all, we need to confess any sin that the Lord brings to our heart and then claim the promise in 1 John 1:9, where he says, "If we confess our sins, he is faithful and just to forgive us our sins, and to cleanse us from all unrighteousness." Second, following confession, praise Him for Who He is. Third, we need to thank Him for what He has done in dying on the cross, and also for the daily blessings which He gives. Fourth, we ought to intercede for the people whom He brings to our minds. One very practical way to do this is to turn to some of the prayers of the apostle Paul, such as are in Philippians 1, and Ephesians 1 and 3, and make those prayers our prayers for our friends. Fifth, we should make petitions for ourselves.

Do you have a time set aside each day? If not, why not start right away? Follow the simple plan suggested. Nothing will take the place of daily devotions.

ASSIGNMENTS

1. Memorize Matthew 6:33 and Philippians 4:13.
2. Set aside fifteen minutes a day for a quiet time.
3. For your own benefit, write down where and when you plan to have your daily quiet time.
4. What do you intend to do during the quiet time? (Be specific in your answer.)

7

THE POWER FOR WITNESSING—
THE HOLY SPIRIT

THIS SEVENTH LESSON covers a most important aspect of witnessing. It concerns the power for witnessing—the Holy Spirit Himself. The biblical basis for this is Acts 1:8: "But ye shall receive power, after that the Holy Ghost is come upon you: and ye shall be witnesses unto me both in Jerusalem, and in all Judea, and in Samaria, and unto the uttermost part of the earth."

Here we have both the promise of power and the assurance that on receiving that power we shall be witnesses unto the Lord Jesus Christ.

We need think only of Peter to realize the need for the power of the Holy Spirit in our lives. Remember how Peter denied the Lord three times, how he was changeable and at times fearful? Then something happened. He was filled with the Holy Spirit, according to the record in Acts. He fear-

lessly preached the Gospel of the Lord Jesus Christ
and declared emphatically that there is "none other
name under heaven given among men, whereby we
must be saved" (Ac 4:12). In response to his message recorded in Acts 2, three thousand people
were added to the Church.

In Acts chapter four, we read of the rise of
persecution against the apostles in those early days.
They came together for a prayer meeting, and Acts
4:29 tells how they prayed: "And now, Lord, behold their threatenings: and grant unto thy servants, that with all boldness they may speak thy
word." The thirty-first verse gives the result: "And
when they had prayed, the place was shaken where
they were assembled together; and they were all
filled with the Holy Ghost, and they spake the
word of God with boldness."

This Is a Spiritual Ministry

We must remember that personal witnessing—
witnessing to another individual for Christ—or for
that matter, any kind of evangelism, is a spiritual ministry. It is a spiritual warfare, a spiritual
battle.

In Ephesians 6:12, God reminds us through the
pen of the apostle Paul: "We wrestle not against
flesh and blood, but against principalities, against
powers, against the rulers of the darkness of this

world, against spiritual wickedness in high places."
According to this same book of Ephesians, every
person who does not know Christ as Saviour is
dead in trespasses and sins (Eph 2:1). A person
outside of Christ is spiritually dead. He is not like
a broken watch which simply needs to be repaired.
He is spiritually dead and must be born again. This
can be accomplished only by the power of the
Spirit of God. It is clear, then, that personal witnessing is a spiritual ministry and includes spiritual
warfare.

Furthermore we learn from 2 Corinthians that
every person outside of Christ is blinded by Satan.
The record is, "The god of this world hath blinded
the minds of them which believe not, lest the light
of the glorious gospel of Christ, who is the image
of God, should shine unto them" (2 Co 4:4). A
person may be ever so brilliant in business and in
the intellectual field, and yet be absolutely blind
concerning the Gospel of the Lord Jesus.

It Is God Who Must Work a Miracle

Man, by wisdom, cannot find God. Man reaches
that goal only by special revelation of the Holy
Spirit; therefore, you and I are utterly dependent
upon the Spirit of God to work a miracle if our
personal witnessing is to be successful and fruitful.

None of us are qualified in ourselves for such

work. No person who has been successful in winning others to Christ can help but feel his insufficiency, inability, and inadequacy. This is, of course, as it ought to be, for we must learn to rely upon the Holy Spirit. Remember this, however, that God needs a spokesman. He could spread the Gospel by angels if He so chose, but He has not. He has chosen you and me. We who know Christ as Saviour are His spokesmen, His ambassadors, His representatives, His witnesses to individuals whom He brings within our daily sphere of influence. We need, therefore, to be filled with the Spirit. In fact the Bible commands that very thing: "And be not drunk with wine, wherein is excess; but be filled with the Spirit" (Eph 5:18).

The Lord Jesus pointed out that we are co-laborers with the Holy Spirit in witnessing. This is what our Lord said, "But when the Comforter is come, whom I will send unto you from the Father, even the Spirit of truth, which proceedeth from the Father, he shall testify of me: and ye also shall bear witness, because ye have been with me from the beginning" (John 15:26-27). The Spirit of truth testifies of the Lord Jesus, and we also bear witness. It is easy to see from this that if we are to be successful, we must be filled with the Holy Spirit.

What Is Involved in This?

What is involved in being filled with the Spirit? There are a number of conditions involved, and one of them is the confession of all our sins. The psalmist said: "If I regard iniquity in my heart, the Lord will not hear me" (Ps 66:18). We can fast, we can stay up all night in prayer, but if we regard any iniquity in our heart, if there is sin there unconfessed, God will not hear us.

One of the memory verses we should know from the chapter "Beginning with Christ" is 1 John 1:9. "If we confess our sins, he is faithful and just to forgive us our sins, and to cleanse us from all unrighteousness." What does it mean to confess our sins? It means to acknowledge them and to call them what God calls them. This is more than a Christian getting on his knees when he goes to bed and saying, "Lord, forgive me for all my sins of today, both of commission and omission." When we confess in the true sense of that word, He promises to forgive us our sins and to cleanse us from all unrighteousness. Then we will have what Paul calls "a conscience void of offence toward God, and toward men."

Let us ask ourselves this very moment, Do we have a conscience void of offence toward God and man? Is there some known sin in our lives uncon-

fessed and unforsaken? If so, let us stop right now
and confess and acknowledge it to Him. That is
one of the great secrets of being filled with the Holy
Spirit.

Next is the complete surrender of the will to
follow Christ. You recall that in our first lesson we
referred to Matthew 4:19, where the Lord Jesus
said, "Follow me, and I will make you fishers of
men." The command is for us to follow Him, then
He will make us fishers of men. It is our responsibility to do the following, and His to teach us to
be fishers of men. To follow Him involves a surrender of our own wills; for if any man will come
after Him, let him deny himself and take up his
cross daily and follow Him. To deny self means to
say no to ourselves, and yes to Him.

Would a young woman who was about to be
married please her prospective husband if she did
not want to leave home or wished to retain her own
name or wanted to bring her family along to live
with her? Of course she would not! A young man
wants a complete surrender to him. Or, suppose
a young man is called into the army but wants to
retain his employment; would that be satisfactory
to his government? No, he must give himself com-
pletely to his country. This same principle is opera-
tive in the service of Jesus Christ, only more so.
There must be a complete surrender of the will to

follow Him, regardless of what it costs. That is the second condition involved in the basis for power in witnessing—being filled with the Holy Spirit.

The third condition is that we by faith depend upon the person of the Holy Spirit, which means that we step out on the promises, trusting Him implicitly. We take the step out of obedience, believing that the Spirit of God will do for us what He has promised—that is, to guide us to the person who needs our help. This He assuredly will do.

During the Billy Graham Crusade in London several years ago, there was an average of 350 persons who responded to the invitation each night. Among the approximately 2,000 personal workers helping us was Mr. Mendenhall, a former alcoholic. Of the 12 alcoholics who came forward during those meetings, without any prearrangement on our part, the Spirit of God so led that 11 of them were dealt with by Mr. Mendenhall.

The Holy Spirit will also guide us in choosing the right Scripture in each situation. It is both amazing and thrilling to have Him bring to our remembrance the portion suitable to meet a particular need. It is only through Him that the Gospel message will go forth through us in real power. This fact is brought before us in 1 Thessalonians 1:5, where Paul says, "For our gospel came not unto you in word only, but also in power, and in the Holy Ghost, and in much assurance." We rely on the Spirit of God to do this.

Finally we trust the Holy Spirit to glorify Christ as we seek to point a needy soul to the Lord Jesus. In witnessing, you and I can only go so far; then we must step back, as it were, and let the person to whom we are talking go alone with the Holy Spirit so that He can do His work in that one's heart.

Let us examine ourselves. Do we have any known sin unconfessed? Are our wills surrendered to the Lord Jesus Christ? Are we willing to step out in faith, depending upon the Holy Spirit to guide us and give us the power to witness concerning the saving grace of Christ?

Assignment

1. Memorize John 13:34-35.
2. Review daily all the verses you have learned thus far and quote them to someone word for word.
3. List three main reasons why the personal worker must be led by the Holy Spirit.
4. What must be true in a person's life if he is to be Spirit directed?

8

LAY THE GROUNDWORK FOR WITNESSING

THE FIRST THING NECESSARY in laying the groundwork for witnessing is that we pray. There is no substitute for this. It is impossible to be a successful soul-winner apart from constant and fervent prayer. We need to ask the Lord for wisdom so that we will know for which person or persons we should pray. God prepares certain hearts to hear the Gospel, and He does that as we pray.

START PRAYING

The story of Philip and the Ethiopian eunuch is a good example of this. Philip was in the middle of a very successful evangelistic campaign when he was told by God to go to another place. "And the Spirit of God came to Philip, saying, Arise, and go toward the south unto the way that goeth down from Jerusalem unto Gaza. . . . And he arose

and went" (Ac 8:26-27). When he arrived there,
he saw a man who, as he journeyed to his distant
home in his chariot, was reading Isaiah the prophet.
"Then the Spirit said unto Philip, Go near, and join
thyself to this chariot" (v. 29). Philip did so and
was used of God to lead the eunuch to Christ. In
this we see how the Holy Spirit led Philip to a particular individual. God will also lead us with regard to those for whom we should pray.

Usually, the ones whom God has placed within
the sphere of our own personal influence—friends,
relatives, neighbors, and business associates—are
the persons for our personal prayer list. Let us
start praying for them daily, regularly, and fervently.

Some may wonder, What should we ask of God
concerning them? One thing we could ask is that
the hostility or the indifference they may have for
the Gospel of the Lord Jesus might be broken
down. Having prayed in this manner, we will
later find, as we approach them, that the way has
been prepared. Just as an electric eye opens a door
ahead of us, so prayer opens the door for our witnessing.

In the second place, we can pray that the soil of
their hearts will be prepared for the seed of the
Word. It is the Holy Spirit who convicts of sin and
points to the Lord Jesus Christ. The Spirit of God

will do His work in answer to prayer if we pray
specifically and definitely. On this particular point,
it is well to consider thoughtfully John 16:8-11,
where we are told of the ministry of the Holy
Spirit: "And when he is come, he will reprove the
world of sin, and of righteousness, and of judgment: of sin, because they believe not on me; of
righteousness, because I go to my Father, and ye
see me no more; of judgment, because the prince of
this world is judged."

We must pray, too, that the person may be liberated from the power of Satan, that blindness may
be removed from their spiritual eyes. The Bible
says, "The god of this world hath blinded the minds
of them which believe not" (2 Co 4:4). We must
therefore pray for specific individuals and pray
with these definite things in mind. As someone has
said, "Be definite with God, and He will be definite
with you."

Furthermore, we need to pray for courage to
speak for Christ. This fact we have considered in
a previous chapter, but it bears repeating. The
apostles found it necessary to make such a request
to God. "And now, Lord, behold their threatenings: and grant unto thy servants, that with all
boldness they may speak thy word" (Ac 4:29).
These men wanted unembarrassed freedom of
speech in order to proclaim the Word of God.

In that same chapter, we read the answers to this prayer. "And when they had prayed, the place was shaken where they were assembled together; and they were all filled with the Holy Ghost, and they spake the word of God with boldness" (v. 31).

Again we read, "And with great power gave the apostles witness of the resurrection of the Lord Jesus: and great grace was upon them all" (v. 33). We will find that by our praying regularly, daily, and specifically, God will give us boldness to speak for Jesus Christ. Prayer, then, is the first thing needed in laying the groundwork for witnessing. Begin now!

In this connection it is a good thing to make a prayer list consisting of the names of our unsaved friends for whom we are going to pray regularly. Then, as the weeks and the months and the years go by, we will see how God answers our prayers.

FIND THE OPPORTUNITY

Not only must we start praying, but we must use such opportunities for witnessing as come our way. Some person may object by saying, "Well, I don't have many opportunities."

Actually, we need only one. Why should we have two or three opportunities if we have not yet taken advantage of the one that the Lord has given us?

We must ever be on the alert for chances to witness. Most of us see what we are interested in. If we are desirous of taking opportunities to witness for Christ, we will see them. If we are not desirous of doing so, we are not likely to see them.

People all around us today are unhappy. They may have lovely homes, have new cars in the driveway, and be well dressed; and yet this could well be the true situation: "Even in laughter the heart is sorrowful; and the end of that mirth is heaviness" (Pr 14:13). They may be putting smiles on their faces and hiding tears in their hearts. I am convinced that if we could look deep into the souls of people who live in our block or the people who walk by any given intersection in any town or country, we would see in most cases heartache, difficulty, frustration, or fear. Those closest to us often have the greatest needs. So we must be alert for opportunities that the Spirit of God will bring to us.

People are hungry today for something that will satisfy them spiritually. Men of God who have been in the Lord's work for many years tell me that it is easier to talk to men and women about Christ today than at any other time in their experience.

We must learn to be friendly to all. As Proverbs says, "A man that hath friends must show himself friendly." We must follow the example of the Lord Jesus, of whom it was said, "Then drew near unto him all the publicans and sinners for to hear him" (Lk 15:1). The common people heard Him gladly. The publicans and sinners came to hear Him. He was a Friend to all of them. We too should be friendly to all.

We can be friendly without jeopardizing our testimony. We must avoid the "holier than thou" attitude. The Lord Jesus ate with sinners though He was criticized for it. In defense of His actions He said: "They that are whole have no need of the physician, but they that are sick: I came not to call the righteous, but sinners to repentance" (Mk 2:17). A friendly attitude will open up many a door to our witness for Christ.

Added to all this, of course, is living the Christian life. That life lived in the power of the Holy Spirit is a joyful, attractive life. Remember in this connection that Christians are to be the salt of the earth.

The little girl in a Sunday school was asked: "What is salt?"

She said: "Salt is to make people thirsty."

Now, perhaps you and I cannot make people drink, so to speak, but we can make them thirsty for spiritual things by the kind of a life that is filled with joy and victory in the Lord Jesus Christ.

When they turn to Him they will be satisfied (Jn 4:10).

In order to make opportunities, we must demonstrate sincere interest in people and show love for them. It says of the Lord Jesus in Acts 10:38 that He "went about doing good." Someone has commented on that passage: "The Lord Jesus went about doing good, but it seems as if we just go about."

We must ask God to show us ways and means to do good to people. To show our love we may need to visit them. There may be occasions when taking over a batch of cookies or a cake to a neighbor will open a heart to listen to our witness. To be helpful at a time of difficulty or sorrow may create the desired opportunity. Some little, thoughtful courtesy with no strings attached may be what God will use in our contacts with a person. In fishing we must go where the fish are and count no opportunity too small.

In laying the groundwork for witnessing, first, start praying. Second, be alert for every opportunity. Be genuinely friendly and live the kind of a life that makes the Christian life attractive. Demonstrate a sincere interest in others by doing the little, thoughtful courtesies that show your love for them.

1. Memorize Psalm 122:1 and Titus 3:8.
2. Start a prayer list of unsaved friends for whom you are going to pray regularly.
3. List what you consider to be the three most effective means to get an opportunity to witness.
4. List some specific ways that you can find an opportunity for personal witnessing with someone whom you know.

9

THE APPROACH

WE NEED TO KNOW HOW to approach persons with the Gospel. Some may wonder why we have not covered this ground in an earlier lesson. The reason is that we must be prepared. The first eight lessons, when followed, provide that preliminary training.

Adequate preparation is an absolute necessity here. Many have tried to witness for Christ without it and have become discouraged. They did not know how to answer people. Unfamiliar with the Scriptures and lacking the undergirding which a consistent time of fellowship with the Lord produces, they did not prepare the way ahead by prayer. Others have tried with no fruit to show for their efforts. Fruit in the Christian life is the result of first taking root. The Scripture says, "And the remnant that is escaped of the house of Judah shall again take root downward, and bear fruit upward" (Is 37:31). If we are to bear fruit in our lives by way of witnessing to others of Christ and winning them to Him, we must first take root.

How do we take root? One way is by getting into the Word of God and acquiring a working knowledge of it. That is one reason why we have emphasized in the various lessons the importance of committing scripture verses to memory. Those of you who have faithfully fulfilled all the lesson assignments up to this point will have memorized the four verses in the chapter "Beginning With Christ" and most of the verses in the next chapter, "Going on With Christ." You will also have set aside a definite time each day for devotional meditation in the Bible and for prayer. In this way fellowship with Christ will be cultivated.

Another fact which we have tried to emphasize is that we must recognize our own helplessness and inadequacy. We need to learn to depend entirely on the Holy Spirit. We should not feel adequate in ourselves, for as soon as we do, we will stop resting and trusting in the Lord. We should never feel as if we know enough. Many servants of God with much experience in back of them tell us that they do not know enough. It is because they have relied upon the Holy Spirit that they have been greatly used.

GET GOING

Even if you are new at this, if you know Christ and have been diligent in studying these lessons you know enough to begin. You have laid the groundwork by way of preparation in your own life. You have prayed definitely and specifically for an individual to whom you might witness, and you have sought to make opportunities whereby you might approach that person. So we suggest that you get going.

We can talk about personal witnessing, we can hear lectures on it, read books on it, listen to challenges on it, and make all needed preparation; but the fact remains that in order to approach someone, we must get going.

Go where people are. In the great commission our Lord Jesus said, "Go ye into all the world, and preach the gospel to every creature" (Mk 16:15). We are not to sit and wait for people to come to us. We are to go to them. Exodus 4:12 is a good verse for a personal witness to take. The Lord said to Moses, "Now therefore go, and I will be with thy mouth, and teach thee what thou shalt say." We must get going to reach people where they are.

For instance, in the first chapter of John we read how Andrew came to know the Lord (vv.

35-40). Immediately following that event it is said of Andrew, "He first findeth his own brother Simon" (v. 41). He found him. That means he went and looked for him and brought him to Jesus. The next person reached was Philip. "The day following Jesus would go forth into Galilee, and findeth Philip" (v. 43). That could only be done by Jesus going where he was. Following that, "Philip findeth Nathanael" (v. 45). He sought him out and brought him to Jesus.

The first essential in the approach to an individual in witnessing is that we get going. That may mean that we will have to forego some Christian fellowship. It is more enjoyable to spend an hour with a Christian friend with whom we have common interests than it is to go and spend some time with someone who does not know the Lord. Remember, however, the Lord Jesus said, "They that are whole need not a physician; but they that are sick. I came not to call the righteous, but sinners to repentance" (Lk 5:31-32). So we must be on the lookout for opportunities to witness.

A few years ago when I was with the Graham team in the Seattle Crusade, a businessman came forward in one of the services and received Christ as his Saviour. The following Sunday night he went to a church in the city and after the service he walked up to one of the leading elders in the church and said to him, "Did you hear that I received Christ as my Saviour one night last week out at the ball park in one of the meetings?"

The elder answered, "Yes, I heard that you did, and I was certainly delighted to hear it."

The man said to the elder, "Tell me, how long have you and I been associated together in business?"

The elder thought for a moment. 'Twenty-three years I believe."

The other went on to say, "Have you known Christ as Saviour all of the twenty-three years?"

"Yes," was the reply, "I have."

"You know," said the new Christian, "I have admired you very much, but I don't remember your ever talking to me about the Lord Jesus Christ." The elder hung his head as the man continued, "I admired you so much that I felt that if a man could be as fine a man as you and not be a Christian, then I didn't need to be a Christian, either."

You see, this dear man had manifested a good life to his business associate, but he had not gone to him to tell him of the Lord Jesus Christ, who made it possible for him to live that kind of life.

If we are going to be successful witnesses for Christ we must get going. We must get out where the people are who need our help. In other words, if we are going to go fishing, we must go where the fish are.

STUDY THE PERSON

What are we to do when we meet the person that we are going to help? The first thing we must *not* do is to think about ourselves. That is the wrong way to begin. The focus of our attention should be on the person whom we are seeking to win. In this matter of personal witnessing there are two people for us to know. We are to know the Lord Jesus Christ and the person to whom we would make Christ known. So we need to study the person we are trying to help in order to find an opening of some kind to courteously, politely, yet definitely speak to him about his relationship to the Lord Jesus.

Remember this, we do not have to know all the answers. We may fear a little lest those with whom we deal ask us some question that we cannot answer. If they do, we should admit frankly that we do not know the answer to that question. We can add, however, "This I do know. I know what the Lord Jesus Christ has done for me. I know what He means to me." In that way we can keep on the subject of what we do know.

WIN CONFIDENCE

We must study the persons we are seeking to help in order to win their confidence. A good way to do this—in fact, I believe it is a must in successful personal witnessing—is to try to discover what legitimate interests a person has so that we might show an interest in what he is interested in.

I read the other day that at one time D. L. Moody played tennis all afternoon with a young man. He had expected to be "button-holed" by Mr. Moody, but the evangelist threw him off balance and won his confidence by playing tennis with him. Later on Mr. Moody was able to speak to him about the Lord Jesus Christ. We will discover that everybody has some legitimate interest in which we too can show a genuine interest. This is very important if we are to be successful fishers of men.

Another kind of bait that can be used in this matter of witnessing is honest and sincere commendation. We must be sure to avoid flattery, however, because anyone can tell the difference between it and true appreciation. We can find something to commend in almost anyone.

I remember one day I walked into a hotel and noticed that the bellboy had a very distinguished looking mustache. It was a very thin mustache, and I was amazed that he could trim it without shaving it off. A day or two later I stepped up to him and said, "Will you pardon me, but you have a mustache which is about as distinguished looking as any I have ever seen." His face lighted up like a Christmas tree, and from there on it was a very simple matter to strike up a conversation with him about his relationship to the Lord Jesus Christ.

Some kind of bait, then, is needed. It may be the other person's interest, some honest and sincere commendation, or as is mentioned in the previous lesson, some thoughtful service and courtesy.

Have you ever asked the Lord to give you some idea for a service that you could perform for a friend, not with the idea that he will be indebted to you, but simply to show your interest and love for him? If you are earnest and sincere, the Lord will show you something that you can do to win that person's confidence and thus win a hearing for the message that you wish to bring.

A wonderful way to win another's confidence is just by the power of a simple testimony as to what the Lord Jesus means to us. Psalm 107:2 says, "Let the redeemed of the LORD say so, whom he hath redeemed from the hand of the enemy." As has already been said, we do not need to know all the answers. We can be like the man in John 9, who had been healed of his blindness by the Lord Jesus and was asked by the Pharisees whether or not Jesus was a sinner. The man answered, "Whether he be a sinner or no, I know not. One thing I know, that, whereas I was blind, now I see" (Jn 9:25). We can say to someone who asks us a question which stumps us: "Well, I don't know the answer to that question, but I know one thing, and that is Jesus Christ has changed my life." The power of that simple testimony will win confidence and a hearing for the wonderful, blessed message that we wish to bring.

ASSIGNMENTS

1. Memorize 2 Corinthians 9:7 and Psalm 107:2.
2. Write out in brief your own testimony so that you could give it in five minutes.
3. What two persons must we know in order to witness effectively?
4. What thoughtful services or courtesies might you render to some non-Christian friend of yours?

10

TELLING THE STORY

THERE ARE THREE THINGS to be covered in this lesson. The first one deals with the Gospel story. The second is concerned with some dos and don'ts in telling the story. The third emphasizes the need of our presenting the true Gospel story to those we are seeking to win for Christ.

GETTING THE OPENING

How can we get an opening to tell the story? This is not an easy question to answer, for there is no formula or infallible rule that we can give. There are, however, some specific suggestions that will help us to get an opening so that we can share the Gospel of the Lord Jesus Christ with another individual. One suggestion is that we use an appropriate, attractive-looking Gospel tract. There are many good Gospel tracts available, but rather than just shoving one into a person's hand, we can approach him something like this: We might say, "Here's something that I would like you to read. It is well worth a thinking person's time. Read it over, and then later on I will ask you what you think about it." We should use some such approach to show to the person with whom we are dealing that behind our handing him a tract is our own personal interest in his eternal welfare.

Another way to find an opening is simply to ask permission to speak about the Lord Jesus Christ. We could say, "May I tell you about something that has meant more to me than anything else in my life?" This will open up a way in a manner that will show courtesy and thoughtfulness to the person to whom we would speak.

I remember an experience I had when I lived in Seattle, Washington. In order to reach my office I had to use an elevator. One day I said to the operator, "Polly, you know I have told you about my wife and family and how much they mean to me. But I feel a little sad about something, and it's this. I have found something that means more to me than married life, more to me than being a father, and I haven't told you about it."

She asked, "What is it?"

I answered, "Well, I'm afraid if I start to tell you now you will get another call. But sometime when you have fifteen minutes I would like to share with you that which means more than anything else in life to me." You can well imagine that she had fifteen minutes on her next lunch hour, which gave me a wonderful opportunity to present the Gospel of the Lord Jesus.

We can see from this that if we have our own personal testimony clearly in mind, that we can share it with another person. This is an effective way to make an opening for telling others what the Lord Jesus means to us.

In one of the previous lessons we saw from Acts 22:14-15 that witnessing is simply taking a good look at the Lord Jesus Christ and then telling others what we have seen. We are to take time to look and listen that we might share with others what we have seen and heard of the Lord Jesus. But whatever we do, as we look to the Lord to give an opening to share the Gospel, we must always be courteous.

Thoughtfulness and courtesy are always in order. A key passage on this subject is 2 Timothy 2:24-25: "And the servant of the Lord must not strive; but be gentle unto all men, apt to teach, patient, in meekness instructing those that oppose themselves; if God preadventure will give them repentance to the acknowledging of the truth." To be courteous and gentle does not mean to be devious. Rather, we should come straight to the point. My own experience in personal witnessing in recent years has convinced me that people appreciate it if we tell them straight from the shoulder what Jesus Christ means to us. They do not care so much for the back-door, devious method of approach.

Then, when we get to the point, stick to the point. Do not let somebody distract us by saying, "Well, what about the contradictions in the Bible? Where did Cain get his wife?" If we cannot show them where Cain got his wife, we could say, "I don't know the answer to that, but I am sure there must be one. Here, however, is something I do know. I know that the Lord Jesus Christ can change a life. He has changed mine. I know what it means to walk with Him daily." We must bring them back to the person of Christ. A study of the fourth chapter of the Gospel of John discloses that in our Lord's dealing with the woman at the well, He had to bring her back to the main point several times, for she tried in various way to sidetrack Him. So, stick to the point.

SOME DOS AND DON'TS

Here are some things to do and some things not to do as we present the Gospel story. We should not presuppose a negative reply. I fear that many of us approach a person about the Lord Jesus Christ and the Gospel, assuming that he is going to disagree with us. Somehow or other that attitude on our own part calls forth a negative response on his part. We should, instead, assume a positive response, knowing that deep down in that person's heart the Holy Spirit will produce the conviction that what we say is the truth. The one we are dealing with may not outwardly admit it, but the conviction will be there nevertheless.

Consider now some things we should do. We must bring people face to face with the person of Jesus Christ. Remember it is Christ who saves, not a theory, not even a system of doctrine. So we must be certain to bring them face to face with Jesus Christ Himself.

As soon as we are into the interview, we need to use our Bibles. Show them from the Bible what God has to say. Turn from one Scripture to another as the need indicates. This provides the Holy Spirit a weapon to use to pierce their hearts. As we noted once before, the Bible is the seed which we are to plant in the soil of their hearts. The Holy Spirit will then work a miracle and give the increase. Moreover, as we use the Word of God in this way we will see to a greater degree the importance of memorizing Scripture.

We must not try to force a decision from a person. This is the work of the Holy Spirit. The new birth is a miracle, and we cannot produce it.

Another thing to avoid is argument. As soon as we start an argument, the other person stops listening to us and just waits for us to finish so that he can make a statement.

Furthermore, keep the message simple. Our Saviour used no hard-to-understand language when He said concerning His mission to this world, "The Son of man is come to seek and to save that which was lost" (Lk 19:10).

PRESENTING THE GOSPEL

Finally, and above all, be sure that we share with them the Gospel. There are many messages which I have heard—supposedly Gospel messages— that have not proclaimed the Gospel in my judgment. The Gospel concerns a certain body of facts. It is the Gospel that is the power of God unto salvation. It is to the Gospel and the facts of the Gospel that Satan has blinded people's minds.

Just what is the Gospel? I know of no better definition than that which is given in 1 Corinthians 15:3-4: "For I delivered unto you first of all that which I also received, how that Christ died for our sins according to the scriptures; and that he was buried, and that he rose again the third day according to the scriptures." This is God's definition of the Gospel. So, whatever else we say in personal witnessing, let us be sure that we present the Gospel.

ASSIGNMENT

1. Review your verses.
2. Enroll in a topical memory system.
3. What are some reasons why argumentation does not work in individual witnessing?
4. How far do you think you should go in trying to answer the doctrines of cults?

11

THE STORY TO TELL

To STRESS FIRST TO A PERSON that he should not wait until tomorrow to receive Christ is not necessarily giving him the Gospel. What we are doing in that case is emphasizing the urgency of his decision with reference to the message of life. It is very important in personal witnessing that we clearly present the facts of the Gospel itself, because, as we learned before, it is concerning these facts that Satan has blinded the minds of men and women. The Bible says, "In whom the god of this world hath blinded the minds of them which believe not, lest the light of the glorious gospel of Christ, who is the image of God, should shine unto them" (2 Co 4:4).

THE CONDITION OF THE LOST

This truth is verified in Acts 26:18, where we are told that a person outside of Christ is blinded, is in darkness, and is under the power of Satan. We learn from Ephesians 2:1 that a person outside of Christ is dead in trespasses and sin—spiritually dead.

What is the remedy for this condition? How can a person be brought from darkness to light, from the power of Satan unto God, from spiritual death unto life, from spiritual blindness to spiritual sight?

THE ONLY REMEDY

We have a remedy, and one only—the Gospel of the Lord Jesus Christ. The key passage on this is Romans 1:16. Here the apostle Paul declares, "For I am not ashamed of the gospel of Christ: for it is the power of God unto salvation to every one that believeth; to the Jew first, and also to the Greek."

WE ARE TO PREACH THE GOSPEL

It is clear then that in our individual witnessing or in any kind of evangelism, we must preach the Gospel. Neither our opinions about the Bible nor even our own experience, though it can be used as illustrative material, is the power of God. Only the Gospel of Christ is that. And only as we give out the message in simplicity and in the power and conviction of the Holy Spirit will souls be saved.

What Is the Gospel?

The scriptural definition of the Gospel is given in 1 Corinthians 15:3-4, "For I delivered unto you first of all that which I also received, how that Christ died for our sins according to the scriptures; and that he was buried, and that he rose again the third day according to the scriptures." These constitute the essential facts of the Gospel. Christ died for our sins according to the Scriptures. He was buried and rose again the third day according to the Scriptures.

The approach to the Scriptures will vary in different instances, but for the sake of illustration and clarification, let us analyze the Gospel message under the following four points.

Sin is a fact

The fact of sin is brought out by such a Scripture passage as Romans 3:23: "For all have sinned, and come short of the glory of God." Having read or quoted this verse to the person to whom we are witnessing, we might then ask, "Does this mean that everyone has sinned but you and me?" The answer is obvious. The statement includes all— all have sinned and come short of the glory of God. True, there are some people who in the eyes of men are more moral than others, but the fact remains that all have come short. We will not argue the point as to whether or not some have come closer. The point is that all have come short.

Suppose, for instance, that we stood on the edge of a chasm, some five hundred feet deep. The distance across is such as to require a thirty-five-foot jump to clear it. Now, the world's record for the broad-jump is something like twenty-eight feet or thereabouts, but that does not deter some persons from trying to cross. A man comes to the edge of the chasm, peers over; sees the five-hundred-foot drop to the rocks below; looks across to the other side, which is thirty-five feet away, and decides to try to jump across. He staggers back a few steps and springs out about five feet, and down he falls. We would say he came short. A little while later an upstanding, moral young man, a keen athlete, looks over the chasm and sees the five hundred-foot drop, looks at the thirty-five feet across, and decides that he will try to jump it to reach the other side. So, after getting back and getting a good run for it, we will say that he breaks the world's record by leaping thirty-one feet; but he too comes short. Admittedly, he came closer, but still he came short.

Since all of us have sinned and come short of the glory of God, then all of us are sinners.

THE PENALTY OF SIN IS DEATH

"For the wages of sin is death" Paul declares in Romans 6:23. God hates sin because it is sin that has robbed us of so much. Every heartache, every sorrow, every difficulty that besets us in this world today—all are ultimately traceable to sin. God wants us to be filled with joy and peace and happiness; therefore, He hates sin and has decreed the penalty of sin to be death. He does not say that the penalty for sin is to live a good life, for certainly we should try to do that. He does not say that the penalty for sin is to go to church regularly; for that, too, we should do. No, the penalty for sin is death. Either you must pay the penalty for your sin, and I must pay the penalty for my sin, or someone else must pay it for us; but the penalty must be paid!

CHRIST PAID THE PENALTY

The Good News of the Bible is that Christ paid the penalty for the sins of us all. One of the many passages on this subject is Romans 5:8, "But God commendeth his love toward us, in that, while we were yet sinners, Christ died for us." Christ paid the penalty of death. He was our Substitute. He took our place.

Point out to the person to whom you are witnessing that only Christ could pay that penalty. It could be stated in this fashion: "I could not pay for your sins, nor could you pay for mine; because I have my sins to think of, and you have yours. If someone is to pay the penalty for us, it will have to be someone who had no sin of his own. The only sinless Person who ever walked this earth was the Lord Jesus Christ. Peter says of Him: 'Who did no sin, neither was guile found in his mouth' (1 Pe 2:22). So, only the Lord Jesus could pay for our sins, since He had none of His own.

"Have you ever wondered how it is that one person could pay the penalty for the sins of all the people who ever lived, are now living, or will live? That person would have to be worth more than the total of all humanity. Do you know anyone like that? Well, God is worth more than all the people who ever lived, are now living, or will live.

"Who is Jesus Christ? God manifested in human flesh. That is why Peter could say, as recorded in Acts 4:12: 'Neither is there salvation in any other: for there is none other name under heaven given among men, whereby we must be saved.' In another place we read of Him: 'Who his own self bare our sins in his own body on the tree' (1 Pe 2:24). Jesus paid the penalty for us."

WE MUST ACCEPT

We must receive this fact. It benefits us only as we appropriate it. Many persons with whom we speak concerning this matter will agree that they are sinners and that the penalty of sin is death. Furthermore, they will at least say that they realize the Lord Jesus paid the penalty for them. They have never benefited from that fact, however; it has not yet given them peace and assurance. The reason is that more than acknowledging the fact is necessary. They must appropriate it.

Perhaps this illustration will clarify this important point. Suppose that we have been invited to a good dinner. Perhaps fried chicken, mashed potatoes, gravy, and some savory green vegetable are on the plates before us. We look at the delicious meal, and each one of us says, "My, I'm hungry. I don't believe I've ever been so hungry before." Yet we sit there and talk about the vitamins and calories in the various foods, while the food gets cold and we starve.

Then someone comes along and says, "Why don't you eat? You do not benefit from food by just looking at it and discussing it!" Of course, we do not. We must eat. So it is with the Lord Jesus. We must take Him for ourselves. We must appropriate Him.

"Well," someone asks, "how do I do that?" The

answer is found in John 1:12: "But as many as received him, to them gave he power [or, the right] to become the sons of God, even to them that believe on his name." We are to receive Him as our own personal Saviour, putting our trust in Him.

Remember also that receiving Him involves repentance. One cannot be saved without repenting. To repent means to change one's mind about God and about sin and to turn from sin in faith to God.

In John 1:13 we read: "Which were born, not of blood [that is, not by inheritance], nor of the will of the flesh [not by self-effort], nor of the will of man [not by trusting some person], but of God." So, we turn from these things and by faith receive the Lord Jesus Christ in our hearts.

I think one verse that clarifies this better for me than any other is Revelation 3:20: "Behold, I stand at the door, and knock: if any man hear my voice, and open the door, I will come in to him, and will sup with him, and he with me." He promises that if I receive Him into my heart He will come in and live with me.

These, then, are the four facts of the Gospel: (1) the fact of sin; (2) the penalty of sin, which is death; (3) Christ paid that penalty; and (4) we must receive Him into our hearts.

ASSIGNMENTS

1. Memorize some of the Scriptures referred to in this chapter.
2. What are some of the things that characterize the condition of a person outside of Christ?
3. Write out in your own words how you would lead a person to Christ.

12

CARING FOR THE NEW CHRISTIAN

WE MUST REMEMBER that when a person comes to know the Lord Jesus as Saviour, that one is born into the family of God as a spiritual baby. He is just a beginner in the Christian life. Therefore, our responsibilities to him are not ended; rather, they have only begun. In fact, there is a sense in which our responsibility is even greater now that he is saved. The situation is similar to that when a baby is born. The parents wait for the day of the little one's birth, but following that event father and mother have work to do—years of it. Of course, the joys and blessings which come to them through the care of their child make the work well worth it all.

So it is when God has given us the opportunity to point someone to Christ and that person has been born again. We have the responsibility as an undershepherd to care for this new Christian.

Now there are certain basic things that new Christians need help on, and some of that help they need immediately. If, for instance, someone should come to know the Lord on Tuesday night, we should not wait until Sunday to begin our follow-up work with him. We should begin right away, on Tuesday night. Then we should seek to be with him again on Wednesday and continue encouraging and instructing him throughout the week.

ASSURANCE

The first essential point to cover would be assurance of salvation. How do we know that we are children of God? How does anyone know that he belongs to the Lord Jesus Christ? We can be certain of this: one of Satan's most used tools is doubt, and he will try to bring it into the life of this new Christian sooner or later.

In past years, as I have taught various groups in personal work or counseling, I have asked how many of them have had at least one doubt arise in their minds as to whether or not they were born again. In every instance the majority of hands went up. Since doubt is a common tool of the enemy, we need to forewarn and to prepare the young Christian to meet it.

There are two main reasons, it seems to me, why persons allow doubts to come into their hearts to rob them of assurance of salvation. (We are assuming, of course, that these persons have really been born again.) The first reason is that too much trust is put in feelings, and they really have nothing to do with salvation. Feelings are not safe guides, for they come and go, being governed largely by our physical condition.

I have talked with many a young Christian, and a favorite question of mine is, "How do you know that the Lord Jesus lives in your heart?" Very often the answer is given in this form: "Well, I certainly feel better." My reply might be something like this: "I am delighted that you feel better, but your feelings may leave. There is something far better than trusting in feelings for the assurance of your salvation."

A second reason for lack of assurance, it seems to me, is that Christians fail to realize we can know we are saved. Those who have followed this course of study faithfully and have fulfilled each assignment will have committed to memory 1 John 5:11-12. These verses relate to assurance of salvation: "And this is the record, that God hath given to us eternal life, and this life is in his Son. He that hath the Son hath life." Do you have the Lord Jesus Christ in your heart? Did you receive Him into your heart by faith? If so, you have the Son; and if you have the Son, you have eternal life.

The verse which follows says, "These things have I written unto you that believe on the name of the Son of God; that ye may know that you have eternal life." You need not guess; you need not hope; you may know. You may be absolutely certain!

As a further illustration, let us consider Revelation 3:20, the verse with which we closed our last lesson. Here we see the Lord Jesus standing at the door of the heart and knocking. Then a plea is made and an assurance given: "If any man hear my voice, and open the door, I will come in to him, and will sup with him, and he with me." I often ask, when dealing with someone about Christ, if he realizes that the Lord Jesus is standing at the door of his heart. When the answer is yes, I say, "Well, how do you know?"

"Well, He says so; 'Behold, I stand at the door and knock.' "

"If He is knocking at your heart's door, what does He want?"

"He wants to come in."

I then point out that Christ will not force His way in. He is waiting to be invited. That is just what this verse says, "If any man hear my voice, and open the door," that is, if we ask Him to come into our hearts and lives, He will accept our invitation. The words are, "I will come in to him."

Then I say something like this, "If you have

never received the Lord Jesus into your heart, but right now you ask Him to enter, do you think He will do so?"

The person may answer, "I don't think so," or "I don't know."

In that case I would go over the verse again and say, "Well, let's look at it once more. 'Behold, I stand at the door, and knock: if any man hear my voice, and open the door, I will come in to him, and I will sup with him [that is, I will live with him], and he with me.' If you ask the Lord Jesus to come into your heart and life right now, do you think He will come in?"

"Well, yes, I think He will."

"How do you know He will?"

"Because He said He would."

That is the answer! You stake your life—in fact your soul—for eternity on the promise of the Lord Jesus. How do I know He came into my heart years ago? Because He promised He would. There are other evidences, but the basic reason for my assurance of salvation lies in the fact that I received Christ by faith, and I am resting upon the promises of His Word.

So, in our care for new Christians, we should see to it that they are grounded immediately on the Word of God, on the assurance of salvation.

Beginning Follow-up Immediately

What is our next responsibility to a new Christian? We must begin follow-up immediately. By follow-up we mean giving personal, spiritual care to the new Christian. Just as a baby needs immediate care, so does each new member born into God's family. We are born into it as babies, not as spiritual adults, as we have already seen. There is no spiritual pill that we can give a new Christian to make him grow to spiritual maturity overnight. Instead, God intends that we all should grow in grace and in the knowledge of our Lord Jesus Christ (2 Pe 3:18).

Now, a baby needs to be fed, protected, and trained. In order that this might be accomplished, a baby needs a parent. A new Christian, a spiritual baby, needs a parent as well.

The apostle Paul considered himself a spiritual parent to those whom he had led to Christ. He wrote, "For though ye have ten thousand instructors in Christ, yet have ye not many fathers: for in Christ Jesus I have begotten you through the gospel" (1 Co 4:15).

It is true that we commit a spiritual baby to God, but He also commits it to us. For example, my wife and I have six children, and we have committed them one by one to the Lord. But the Lord also has committed them to us. If our children are not properly fed and protected and trained, we cannot blame God for it, nor can we blame our children. That responsibility we must take ourselves. So it is with new Christians. They must be fed and taught how to feed themselves from the Bible. They must be protected from the false doctrines and other attacks of the enemy that will come. Young believers need to be trained so that they in turn might reach others for Christ and be spiritual parents to them. All of this involves time and care and prayer and work.

It is evident from this that what happens to young Christians depends on how well they are cared for by us who have had the privilege of leading them to Christ. Another reason young believers need immediate care is that Satan attacks them with doubts, temptations and discouragements.

How to Help the Christian

It was because of our awareness of Satan's methods that we prepared the booklet *Beginning with Christ*, formerly called *B Rations*. In this we take up the three major attacks of Satan on the young Christian and show how these attacks can be met. And it is for this same reason that we have asked you to read it carefully and to commit the Bible verses in it to memory. You will be helped in your own spiritual life, and you will have something that will help the person whom you have led to the Lord.

ASSIGNMENTS

1. Review twelve weeks of notes.
2. Make sure you know your verses word for word.
3. List some evidences that we might expect in the life of a person who has made a sincere decision for Christ.
4. Are we right in assuming that when a convert does not go on he was insincere? State reasons.

13

CONTINUING THE CARE OF THE NEW CHRISTIAN

DAILY PRAYER FOR THE ONE COUNSELED

IT IS VERY IMPORTANT that we pray daily for the person whom we have helped to know Christ. The prayers of the apostle Paul found in Philippians 1:9-11, in Colossians 1:9-11, in Ephesians 1 and in Ephesians 3 show what he prayed for with reference to those for whom he had spiritual responsibility. In one place he said,

> For this cause I bow my knees unto the Father of our Lord Jesus Christ, of whom the whole family in heaven and earth is named, that he would grant you, according to the riches of his glory, to be strengthened with might by his Spirit in the inner man; That Christ may dwell in your hearts by faith; that ye, being rooted and grounded in love, may be able to comprehend with all saints what is the breadth, and length, and depth, and height;

And to know the love of Christ, which passeth knowledge, that ye might be filled with all the fullness of God" (Eph 3:14-19).

Meditate on these requests. They show what is necessary in the lives of all Christians.

In writing to the Thessalonians Paul declared how often he prayed for fellow believers: "Night and day praying exceedingly that we might see your face, and might perfect that which is lacking in your faith" (1 Th 3:10). We, too, should pray daily, consistently, and fervently for the persons whom we have been privileged to point to the Lord Jesus Christ.

CONTACTING NEW CHRISTIANS

We should get together with new Christians within twenty-four or forty-eight hours at the most. As we prayerfully repeat the visit, we will discover that the enemy has already been at work. Doubts will have arisen, questions will have come to their minds, problems will have risen at home or at work concerning their new-found faith. They will need the warmth of our personal touch and our continuing interest. We will need to put ourselves out to do everything possible for their spiritual good. When we visit them we should have a time of prayer and try to help them meet their problems by instructing them further in the Scriptures. The

Lord will help us in this if we look to Him. A telephone call between visits, inquiring concerning their progress, will encourage them.

If we are unable to contact them by a visit or by a phone call, we can write a letter. Too often, however, we put off writing a letter until we can write one that we think is long enough, not realizing that a brief letter of encouragement would be better. To write frequently, even though briefly, is what is needed. Many of us do not realize the power of a personally penned letter in which we pour out our heart as we seek to be of assistance to the person whom we have led to Christ.

I remember an incident which occurred a couple of years ago when we were in London with the Billy Graham team. One of our fine, personal-work counselors, Mrs. Mendenhall, spoke with a Dutch woman one night. She did not receive the Lord then. Something just was not clear to her. Mrs. Mendenhall did not give up, however. She went home, and before she retired, she poured out her heart in a letter to the Dutch woman, explaining again as carefully as she could the Gospel message.

When the Dutch woman received the letter, she read it over very carefully, then knelt down and received the Lord Jesus Christ as her own personal Saviour. She did not keep the letter to herself but circulated it among her friends. Within three months, ten of them had come to know Christ as personal Saviour through reading the letter. Altogether too often we do not realize the power of a written testimony. We need to make more use of this method of witnessing.

WHAT TO DO?

Here are two additional suggestions for helping new Christians. After having studied this matter for some years and having specialized in the care of new Christians, I have come to the conviction that one of the most helpful things we can do for them is to get them to commit scripture verses to memory. In that way the Holy Spirit has a weapon, the Word, that He can call to their minds at any time and anywhere.

I suggest that we introduce new Christians to the booklet *Beginning with Christ*, either our own copy or one we secure for them. When they have committed to memory the four verses which are in it, then have them use the booklet *Going On With Christ*. After they have memorized the eight verses of *Going On With Christ*, encourage them to enroll in the Topical Memory System Correspondence Course.

The Topical Memory System has in it 108 verses, topically arranged. These are not sent all at once but in units. With each unit of well-selected verses there is a guidebook with a progress test, which not only suggests particular verses to memorize but also teaches how to successfully commit scripture verses to memory. To repeat what I have written before in these lessons, nothing has paid greater dividends for me than the time spent in committing Scripture to memory.

That, however, is not the only way to come to know the Bible. We should encourage new Christians to read it consistently and consecutively for themselves. We often suggest the gospel of John because it goes into the life of the Lord Jesus and shows so clearly how to be saved. I might suggest also Mark and the book of 1 Thessalonians, which was written to very young Christians.

Furthermore, we must see to it that they become active in the fellowship of a good, Bible-believing church. God wants us to hide the Word on the tables of our heart through memorizing it; He wants us to read it; but He also wants us to hear it preached.

He tells us in Jeremiah 3:15: "And I will give you pastors according to mine heart, which shall feed you with knowledge and understanding." It may be that we will have to call for the new Christians on Sunday mornings and take them to Sunday school and church. God does not intend that we try to get along without the fellowship of other

Christians and the fellowship of a Bible-believing, Gospel-preaching church (Heb 10:24-25).

REMEMBER

As I have suggested, we should visit with our young Christians regularly and pray with them, not depending on the Sunday fellowship to be sufficient for them. We ought to contact them during the week, perhaps have lunch with them. They need our help to not only know the Bible through memorizing Scripture, through Bible reading, and through Bible study, but they need to be taught how to have a daily quiet time. We should share with them some of the wonderful things that God has taught us. In all of this, of course, we are preparing them for the day when they, in turn, will share with others—their neighbors and their friends—what Christ has done for them. God wants new Christians to grow, and to become effective personal witnesses. They can reproduce spiritually by sharing their knowledge of Christ and spiritual truth with others. But in order to do this, they must have continuing help from us.

In conclusion, I would like to summarize all thirteen lessons of this course in just four verses of Scripture. The first is Matthew 4:19. Here we read that when the Lord Jesus called several of His disciples, He said, "Follow me, and I will make you fishers of men." Do you want to be a fisher of men? You can be if you will but follow. The command is to follow Him, and His promise is that He will make us fishers of men.

The second is Acts 22:14-15. Paul, in giving his testimony before the multitude in Jerusalem, repeated the words of Ananias: "The God of our fathers hath chosen thee, that thou shouldest know his will, and see that Just One, and shouldest hear the voice of his mouth. For thou shalt be his witness unto all men of what thou hast seen and heard." In other words, we are to take time to look at the Lord Jesus and to listen to what He has to say to us through His Word, the Bible. Then we can go out and witness to others of what we have seen and heard. Have you been taking time to look and to listen?

The third passage reads, "Ye shall receive power, after that the Holy Ghost is come upon you: and ye shall be witnesses unto me" (Ac 1:8). This is the promise of the power of the Holy Spirit for witnessing.

The fourth and final passage is Exodus 4:10-12. When Moses said to the Lord, "O my Lord, I am not eloquent neither heretofore . . . but I am slow of speech, and of a slow tongue," the Lord asked him, "Who hath made man's mouth?" Then He commanded "Now therefore go, and I will be with thy mouth, and teach thee what thou shalt say."

ASSIGNMENTS

1. What are some things you might do personally to encourage and help a new Christian?
2. As you look back over the weeks you have been memorizing Scripture, list some of the outstanding results that have come to your life from these passages.
3. What have been the greatest blessings to your own life as a result of your daily quiet time with the Lord?

14

BEGINNING WITH CHRIST

JESUS CHRIST SAID, "Behold, I stand at the door, and knock: if any man hear my voice, and open the door, I will come in to him, and will sup with him, and he with me" (Rev 3:20). Coupled with this wonderful truth is the statement in His Word that "as many as received him, to them gave he power to become the sons of God" (Jn 1:12).

If you have to the best of your knowledge received Jesus Christ, God's Son, as your own Saviour, according to the Scripture quoted above you have become a son of God in whom Jesus Christ dwells.

Altogether too many people make the mistake of measuring the certainty of their salvation by their feelings. *Do not* make this tragic mistake; believe God. Take Him at His Word: "These things have I written unto you that believe on the name

This chapter, "Beginning with Christ," is from the booklet of the same name published by The Navigators. It is used here with their permission.

of the Son of God; that ye may know that ye have eternal life" (1 John 5:13).

It is impossible in this short space to go into all the wonderful results of the transaction that took place when you received Christ. A child may be born into a wealthy home and may become the possessor of good parents, brothers and sisters, houses and lands, but at the time of his birth the main point is not that he be informed of all these wonderful things. There are other important matters which must be taken care of first. He must be fed; he is hungry and needs to grow. He must be protected, for he has been born into a world of many enemies. In the hospital room he is handled with sterilized gloves and kept from outsiders that he might not fall victim to any of the myriads of germs waiting to attack. It is the knowledge of such enemies on the part of the doctors and nurses which enables them to take measures to protect the precious new life.

You have become a *child of God;* you have been born as a babe into His family. This is a strategic moment in your life. It is our desire to impart to you two or three simple truths that are not difficult to understand, but the knowledge of them will strengthen you for the battle ahead and keep you safe from the wiles of Satan, the enemy of your soul.

In 1 Peter 2:2 you will read, "As newborn babes, desire the sincere milk of the word, that ye may grow thereby." In Acts 20:32 you will read, "And now, brethren, I commend you to *God*, and to the Word of His grace, which is able to build you up." His Word will now serve as food for your soul and will build you up in the faith. Doubtless you have a New Testament. If not, by all means procure one and begin to read it faithfully daily. It is most important that you have time set aside, preferably in the morning, to read and study the Word of God and pray.

Now we want to be even more specific with regard to partaking of the Word of God. In the ninth and eleventh verses of Psalm 119 we read, "Wherewithal shall a young man cleanse his way? by taking heed thereto according to thy word," and then the psalmist speaks to the Lord saying, "Thy word have I hid in mine heart, that I might not sin against thee." So we challenge you to hide it in your heart—to memorize it.

But we have spoken only about food for your soul. Let us consider for a moment the new and deadly enemy whom you face.

In the past you have not been viciously attacked by Satan, but now he has seen you make the step which angers him more, perhaps than any one thing in all the world. You have left him and joined the ranks of those who believe and trust in the Son of God. You are no longer Satan's property, but you belong to the One who has bought and paid for you with a price, the price of His own shed blood on the cross. You may be sure, then, that Satan will attempt to trouble you. His attack assumes many forms, but we wish to speak of some of the most common ones and give you help on how to resist him successfully.

We can overcome him only as we use the weapon which God has provided. Ephesians 6:17 says "Take . . . the sword of the Spirit, which is the Word of God." Not only is the Word of God spoken of as the *sword of the Spirit* but it is that through which faith comes as a shield to ward off the darts of the enemy (Ro 10:17, Eph 6:16). The Word of God, then, is your weapon of defense as well as your weapon of offense.

To illustrate, we would like to point you to the fact that our Lord was tempted by Satan in three ways, and He met each temptation with Scripture, saying, "It is written" (see Matthew 4). If our Lord Jesus Christ deemed it necessary thus to meet Satan, how much more we need this mighty weapon, the Word of God. How much more we need to be prepared to say to Satan, "It is written" or "Thus saith the Lord."

ASSURANCE OF SALVATION

The four passages of Scripture to be memorized will equip you for your first few encounters with the enemy. His first approach is often to cast doubt upon the work which God has wrought in your heart, and although you will not hear his audible voice, he will whisper to your heart: "You don't think you are saved just by believing and receiving Christ? Surely that is not enough to have your sins blotted out, to be born again, to gain entrance to heaven!"

What will your answer be? Your only hope to withstand such an attack is to resort to God's Word. What does God say about the matter? That is the important thing. And so the first one of the four passages, 1 John 5:11-12, entitled "Assurance of Salvation," says,

> And this is the record, that God hath given to us eternal life, and this life is in His Son. He that hath the Son hath life; and he that hath not the Son of God hath not life.

When this passage has been written on the table of your heart so that you are able to use it every time a doubt arises during the next few days, and when, on the basis of this "record," you are thoroughly convinced that you now have the Lord Jesus Christ and with Him eternal life, you will have overcome in one of the first tests. This attack may recur, but now you have in your heart the Word of God with which to meet it.

ASSURANCE OF VICTORY

The second attack of Satan may be along this line. He may whisper to your heart of hearts: "You have life, all right, but you are a weakling; you have always been a weakling, especially in the case of this or that."

He will remind you of some sin which has gripped you throughout the past years of your life. He will point to something of which you are keenly aware, and say: "You are weak; you will not be able to stand against this particular temptation. Perhaps you will be able to stand against others, but not this one."

How will you answer him? Will you attempt to reason? Will you attempt to produce your own arguments? Will you run to see what this person or that one says? Or will you resort to the invincible Word? The second passage, 1 Corinthians 10: 13, is chosen especially to meet this attack of Satan:

> There hath no temptation taken you but such as is common to man: but God is faithful, who will not suffer you to be tempted above that ye are able; but will with the temptation also make a way to escape, that ye may be able to bear it.

This gives the "Assurance of Victory." God promises victory. It belongs to you as a child of His. Believe it, and you will see that those things which are impossible with men are possible with God. It will thrill you to see that chains of lifetime habits are snapped by His mighty power. Memorize this verse; write it on the table of your heart.

ASSURANCE OF FORGIVENESS

We now come to the third attack of Satan. Although victory is rightfully yours, you are likely to see failure at some point. Sin will suddenly crop up, and immediately your enemy will be on the job to say: "Now you've done it. Aren't you supposed to be a Christian? Christians don't do those things."

Nevertheless, God makes provision in His Word for the failures of His children, and so the third passage speaks of the "Assurance of Forgiveness," 1 John 1:9:

> If we confess our sins, he is faithful and just to forgive us our sins, and to cleanse us from all unrighteousness.

Here He not only promises to forgive us but also to cleanse us. What a gracious provision!

ASSURANCE OF PROVISION

The three preceding assurances have been given to meet the principal attacks of Satan. However,

there is one more. Your needs for the future warfare, for living the life, for witnessing, along with
all your personal needs, will doubtless be many.
God assures us that in answer to prayer He will
take care of every need. Hence, the fourth verse
is the "Assurance of Provision," John 16:24:

> Hitherto have ye asked nothing in my name: ask,
> and ye shall receive, that your joy may be full.

When you are able to quote the first verse, tackle
the second in the same way and review the first.
Then, when you are able to quote these two, tackle
the third. When you can repeat the three verses
perfectly, start on the fourth.

By all means remember that the secret of successful memory work is review! *Review!*

After you have memorized these four verses and
applied them according to the instructions, you will
be aware of the strength and blessings that come
from hiding God's Word in your heart. You may
continue a systematic memory program capable of
producing growth in your Christian life.

15

GOING ON WITH CHRIST

WITHOUT A DOUBT you have experienced some of the temptations that confront new Christians, and we hope you have met them through God's appointed means, His Word. First Peter 5:8 describes Satan as a "roaring lion" and cautions us to keep alert for his subtle attacks. Only as you meet each temptation by effectively using God's Word will you be able to overcome the enemy.

We cannot too strongly emphasize that His Word is the source of daily victory for you. To describe fully the part that the Word plays in your daily walk, work, and worship, this chapter would have to become a volume. Let us consider a few of them, however.

It is through God's Word that the following are accomplished:

This chapter, "Going on with Christ," is from the booklet of the same name. It is copyrighted by the Navigators and used with their permission. *Beginning with Christ* and *Going on with Christ* are printed with memory cards in handy carrying cases.

God directs your paths (Ps 119:105).
Your faith is strengthened (Ro 10:17).
You are fed (1 Pe 2:2, 3).
You grow (Ac 20:32).
Joy is brought into your Christian life (Jn 15:11).
Obedience is made possible (Jn 14:21).
You have the means with which to witness (Pr 22:17-18).

Second Timothy 3:16 sums it up by saying that the Scriptures were given to you for "instruction in righteousness."

Privilege is accompanied by responsibility, and so the Bible points out what God expects from us as a result of what He does for us. Many of His promises are given unconditionally, but most of those which have to do with growth, victorious living, fruitbearing, fullness of joy, and the like, may be appropriated only by obedience to the known will of God. In this chapter we consider the responsibility aspect and study selected passages which will play an important part in the foundation for a strong, productive life.

The eight passages to be memorized show some of the first and most important things you should incorporate into your Christian life. Get them into your heart and on the tip of your tongue, so that you may be able to carry out His orders readily. "The word is very nigh unto thee, in thy mouth, and in thy heart, that thou mayest do it" (Deu 30: 14).

PREPARATION FOR VICTORY

God promises you victory at all times. To the Corinthian Christians the Word was: "Thanks be to God, which giveth us the victory through our Lord Jesus Christ" (1 Co 15:57). To the children of God at Thessalonica the promise was: "The Lord is faithful, who shall stablish you, and keep you from evil" (2 Th 3:3). Through His servant Jude He said, "He is able to keep you from falling, and to present you faultless before the presence of his glory with exceeding joy" (Jude 24).

Is this the experience of all Christians? Unfortunately, no. Not because God does not desire it, but because so many do not realize their part in heart preparation and in appropriation of these wonderful promises. What does God's Word teach as to your part in the victorious life? The answer is seen in the book of Psalms in the Old Testament, and the passage we recommended for your memory is Psalm 119:9, 11: "Wherewithal shall a young man cleanse his way? by taking heed thereto according to thy word. . . .Thy word have I hid in mine heart, that I might not sin against thee." As you memorize this passage, you will more clearly understand how the Word of God strengthens your life and enables you to be kept from sin.

First Things First

God promises to provide for every need of your life. The Philippian church was assured: "God shall supply all your need according to his riches in glory by Christ Jesus" (Phil 4:19). Christ, in preparing His disciples for times of hardship, told them that their heavenly Father was already aware of their needs: "For your Father knoweth what things ye have need of before ye ask him" (Mt 6:8). In Psalm 37:3-4 we read, "Trust in the Lord, and do good; so shalt thou dwell in the land, and verily thou shalt be fed. Delight thyself also in the Lord; and he shall give thee the desires of thine heart."

How does this apply to you? As you determine to know Him better—putting Him, His will, and His work first—you will find that there will be no cause for concern about any of your needs. In memorizing Matthew 6:33, remember that the promise is dependent upon your obedience to the first part: "But seek ye first the kingdom of God, and his righteousness; and all these things shall be added unto you."

How It Can Be Done

The God of all power, whose child you are, assures you of strength for your daily life. Seeming failure on your part to carry out God's desires could be used by Satan to discourage you. You may feel totally inadequate to live the victorious Christian life, yet to you come the comforting words of 2 Corinthians 12:9: "My grace is sufficient for thee: for my strength is made perfect in weakness."

Many years ago God said to His children—and the promise is just as clear and sure today—"Fear thou not; for I am with thee: be not dismayed; for I am thy God: I will strengthen thee; yea, I will help thee; yea, I will uphold thee with the right hand of my righteousness" (Is 41:10).

When the Lord Jesus was with His disciples the last night, He said, "I am the vine, ye are the branches: he that abideth in me, and I in him, the same bringeth forth much fruit: for without me ye can do nothing" (Jn 15:5). In that very sentence, He indicated that with His presence in their lives they could accomplish anything. And so we direct your attention to Philippians 4:13 as one of the deciding factors in the strong, yielded life: "I can do all things through Christ which strengtheneth me."

Love, the Answer

Love is without a doubt the strongest force in the universe. It was love that caused God to deliver His Son as a sacrifice for our sins: "But God commendeth his love toward us, in that, while we were yet sinners, Christ died for us" (Ro 5:8). It is His love and compassion for His children that underlies His tenderness and mercy in forgiving them their sins: "Thou hast in love to my soul delivered it from the pit of corruption: for thou hast cast all my sins behind thy back" (Is 38:17).

Besides being one of the greatest themes throughout the Word, love is a subject to which an entire chapter is devoted. This chapter, 1 Corinthians 13, does not reiterate the great truths of God's love for you as much as it challenges you to let love be the motivating force in your life. He knows that if love is the controlling factor in your life, the greatest problems of living for and working with other people will be solved. That is why He enjoins fervent love for others: "And above all things have fervent [love]* among yourselves: for [love]* shall cover the multitude of sins" (1 Pe 4: 8). This was so essential that the Lord Jesus said to His disciples, "A new commandment I give unto you, That ye love one another; as I have loved you, that ye also love one another. By this shall all men know that ye are my disciples, if ye have love one to another" (Jn 13:34-35). Write this great truth on the table of your heart, and ask God to help you demonstrate it in your daily life.

*The word "charity" in the KJV means "love."

YOU AND THE CHURCH

God's appointed means of establishing the believer in the Christian walk and life is the church. Here the Christian will receive "instruction in righteousness" through the Word that is preached. Here God's appointed men will feed the newborn Christian with the "milk of the Word" (1 Pe 2: 2). He has said, "I will give you pastors according to mine heart, which shall feed you with knowledge and understanding" (Jer 3:15). In Ephesians 4 we read,

> "And he gave . . . pastors, and teachers; for the perfecting of the saints, for the work of the ministry, for the edifying of the body of Christ: till we all come in the unity of the faith, and of the knowledge of the Son of God, unto a perfect man, unto the measure of the stature of the fulness of Christ: that we henceforth be no more children . . . but speaking the truth in love, may grow up into him in all things, which is the head, even Christ" (vv. 11-15).

At the same time, association with other believers and those of like mind is extremely important, because it is in the church that His children have fellowship one with another. In fact, we are commanded thus to meet in Hebrews 10:25: "Not forsaking the assembling of ourselves together, as the manner of some is; but exhorting one another:

and so much more, as ye see the day approaching." We are sure that as you realize His will for you, your response will be like that of David: "I was glad when they said unto me, Let us go into the house of the Lord" (Ps 122:1).

THE PLACE OF GOOD WORKS

God gives grace equal to every job He asks you to do. Second Corinthians 9:8 assures you, "God is able to make all grace abound toward you: that ye . . . may abound to every good work." You were not saved by your works, but one of the great objectives God has in mind is that your life be filled with good works: "For we are his workmanship, created in Christ Jesus unto good works" (Eph 2:10). Paul's earnest prayer for the Colossian Christians was that their lives might be acceptable to God and then, as a result, be fruitful in every way. "That ye might walk worthy of the Lord unto all pleasing, being fruitful in every good work, and increasing in the knowledge of God" (Col 1:10).

Faithfulness in maintaining good works is your part. Each command you have learned from God's Word is for you to obey. As you learn others, put them into practice. His direction in Titus 3:8 is: "This is a faithful saying, and these things I will that thou affirm constantly, that they which have believed in God might be careful to maintain good works. These things are good and profitable unto men." Not only will God be glorified, but you—and others through you—will profit as you seek to carry out His orders.

GIVING JOYFULLY

God's inexhaustible riches are available to you. As His child you are an heir to all that He possesses, both spiritually and materially: "And if children, then heirs; heirs of God, and joint-heirs with Christ" (Ro 8:17). It was for this purpose that Christ left His glory in heaven and came to earth: "For ye know the grace of our Lord Jesus Christ, that, though he was rich, yet for your sakes he became poor, that ye through his poverty might be rich" (2 Co 8:9). His willingness and eagerness to enrich your life is indicated in Romans 8:32: "He that spared not his own Son, but delivered him up for us all, how shall he not with him also freely give us all things?"

You undoubtedly will want to know how you can bring joy to our Lord in gratitude for what He has done. Here is one important way—one that will also have its effect in helping others. To see in you the same spirit of joyful giving will delight His heart. So we recommend that you write this pas- sage upon your heart: "Every man according as he purposeth in his heart, so let him give; not grudgingly, or of necessity: for God loveth a cheerful giver" (2 Co 9:7).

WITNESSING FOR CHRIST

The greatest of God's marvelous provisions for man is seen in His plan of salvation. By taking our place, Christ paid the full price for our sins and their inevitable results: "Christ hath redeemed us from the curse of the law, being made a curse for us" (Gal 3:13). Your eternal life was made possible at a tremendous cost to our Lord: "Forasmuch as ye know that ye were not redeemed with corruptible things . . . but with the precious blood of Christ" (1 Pe 1:18-19). Because of this, you have been liberated from Satan's power and forgiven of all sin. Ephesians 1:7 shows us that in Him "we have redemption through his blood, the forgiveness of sins, according to the riches of his grace."

What does God expect of you in response to what He has done? The Scriptures say, "Whosoever shall call upon the name of the Lord shall be saved. How then shall they call on him in whom they have not believed? and how shall they believe in him of whom they have not heard?" (Ro 10:13-14). The Gospel story must get out. He needs you to tell this wonderful news to others who have not heard. To you who have been bought with a price He says, "Let the redeemed of the LORD say so, whom he hath redeemed from the hand of the enemy" (Ps 107:2).

Verses to be memorized are Psalm 119:9, 11; Matthew 6:33; Philippians 4:13; John 13:34-35; Psalm 122:1; Titus 3:8; 2 Corinthians 9:7; Psalm 107:2.

AFTER THIS BOOK—WHAT?

Now that you have begun to see the tremendous value of hiding God's Word in your heart, you will undoubtedly want to continue. Scripture memory is more than simply learning verses. There are many problems along the way. These problems and ways and means of overcoming them have been carefully considered in what is known as the Navigators Topical Memory System. Learning the how of Scripture memory as well as the what is also part of this course. This correspondence course is available to help you continue to learn and use the Word of God and can be completed in four to eight months.

For further information, write to The Navigators, Colorado Springs, Colorado.